Legacy

LEGACY

**LIVE WITH PURPOSE.
FIND FULFILLMENT.
BE REMEMBERED.**

MARCUM DAVIS

NEW YORK

LONDON • NASHVILLE • MELBOURNE • VANCOUVER

LEGACY

LIVE WITH PURPOSE FIND FULFILLMENT BE REMEMBERED

Published in New York, New York, by Morgan James Publishing. Morgan James is a trademark of Morgan James, LLC. www.MorganJamesPublishing.com

Scripture quotations marked (NIV) are taken from the Holy Bible, New International Version®, NIV®. Copyright © 1973, 1978, 1984, 2011 by Biblica, Inc.™ Used by permission of Zondervan. All rights reserved worldwide. www.zondervan.comThe "NIV" and "New International Version" are trademarks registered in the United States Patent and Trademark Office by Biblica, Inc.™

Scripture quotations marked (NLT) are taken from the Holy Bible, New Living Translation, copyright ©1996, 2004, 2015 by Tyndale House Foundation. Used by permission of Tyndale House Publishers, Carol Stream, Illinois 60188. All rights reserved.

Taken from the Complete Jewish Bible by David H. Stern. Copyright © 1998. All rights reserved. Used by permission of Messianic Jewish Publishers, 6120 Day Long Lane, Clarksville, MD 21029. www.messianicjewish.net.

Berean Literal Translation

Proudly distributed by Publishers Group West®

A **FREE** ebook edition is available for you
or a friend with the purchase of this print book.

CLEARLY SIGN YOUR NAME ABOVE

Instructions to claim your free ebook edition:
1. Visit MorganJamesBOGO.com
2. Sign your name CLEARLY in the space above
3. Complete the form and submit a photo
   of this entire page
4. You or your friend can download the ebook
   to your preferred device

ISBN 9781636982700 paperback
ISBN 9781636982717 ebook
Library of Congress Control Number:
2023942596

Cover Design by:
Marcum Davis and Michael Aliorde

Interior Design by:
Chris Treccani
www.3dogcreative.net

Morgan James is a proud partner of Habitat for Humanity Peninsula
and Greater Williamsburg. Partners in building since 2006.

Get involved today! Visit: www.morgan-james-publishing.com/giving-back

Dedication

I dedicate this book to my father, Milton Davis. Dad, you've never faltered in your dedication to your family, convictions, or faith. You are one of the rare men who has been married to the same woman for more than sixty years, and your entire career was about ministry and service. Most of all, you've always been a loving guide and supporter to me through all of my adventures. I dedicate this book on legacies to the man who has demonstrated it most to me. I love you, Dad. I'm proud to be your son.

I also dedicate this book to my eternal Father. You loved me even before the foundations of the world. Your presence in my life is beautiful beyond words. You have taken me to places I'd never have dreamed possible. Thank you for everything, literally.

Table of Contents

Is This Your Pivotal Moment?

Something caused you to pick up the book you're holding in your hands. I don't know what it was and, honestly, you might not either.

Sometimes we just get a feeling about a book or a message that piques our curiosity.

With a topic like legacy, your reason could be a number of things.

For some reason, you became curious about or maybe even committed to building your legacy.

For some people, beginning to focus on building a legacy follows a joyful moment, like becoming a parent or grandparent. With others, it comes from life challenges, like an illness or the death of a loved one. Other times, it follows something seemingly inconsequential, like picking up this book after something on the cover caused you to feel *something*, even if you still aren't sure what that feeling is . . .

No matter what the reason, I think of these as our pivotal moments—the moments in our lives when we commit to stop living small and venture purposefully into discovering the person we were created to be.

Even if you don't yet know why you came to be reading this book, I'm honored you're here.

As you'll read over the rest of this book, although I had always been a student of personal and professional growth, the pivotal moment that caused me to become hyperfocused on legacy didn't happen until one month before my fifty-ninth birthday, almost to the day, on February 24, 2022, in the city of Mykolaiv, Ukraine . . .

Introduction:

The Making of a Legacy

If you're going to live, leave a legacy.
Make a mark on the world that can't be erased.
—MAYA ANGELOU

It was 5:30 a.m. on February 24, 2022, when I was woken suddenly by the earth shaking and the sounds of explosions in the distance. The local airport in the city of Mykolaiv, Ukraine, had been destroyed. There was no leaving now, and we knew the Russians were coming.

As an American living and working in Ukraine for most of the previous decade, I had become accustomed to hearing the rattlings of war in the daily news. The stories of military tensions on the border were nothing new. It had seemed to be mostly egos, politics, and posturing, and life went on. Not this time. It was all very real.

Within minutes, I was dressed and heading out to see what was happening on the streets. I will never forget it. Panic gripped the people as they ran to stores, ATMs, and gas stations to prepare for the unknown. No one knew when anything would be restocked, so they grabbed what they could and prepared for the worst.

I picked up some of my staff and headed to the closest orphanage we'd been supporting through my nonprofit organization, Abundance International. The orphanage only had five days of food left to feed more than sixty infants, so we went to work to get them resupplied. I never doubted that I was there for a reason; for such a time as this. I knew there was something I was supposed to do to help. I was driven by an internal sense of mission, and so was my team. We rose to the challenge and met the needs of these children. I'll forever be proud of how everyone worked to help each other in this unprecedented time of crisis. The lessons I learned about being a legacy maker have changed the way I respond to everything.

You may not be called to bring aid to the innocent in a war zone, but I know this for certain—we all come to this world with a mission to discover and live out. We somehow know intuitively that we've been given an assignment, a purpose, a calling that is unique to us. But along the way, we lose focus. The busyness of daily life numbs many people from having to think about it and their passion fades. But for you and me, our need for significance never leaves us.

As Morpheus tells Neo in the movie *The Matrix*, "It's the question that drives us." But our question is not, "What is the Matrix?" Instead, a still, quiet voice inside asks, "What is my purpose for being here?" We ask because we know there is a unique answer for us. But, how to find it?

Times are changing, and we feel like our foundations have been rocked. We ask, "Is this all there is?" The search for meaning, peace, and happiness drives us, but we don't know how to consistently bring it into our daily experience. We make decisions that we later regret because we have no compass; no North Star to guide us. Where are the rock-solid convictions that give us confidence in where we're going and what we are about?

You're not alone. I've struggled for much of my life with that exact same story. I looked for meaning and fulfillment in as many ways as I could, only to feel alone again and living below my potential. But I can tell you that it is possible to find peace and confidence no matter the season of life once you understand how they all make sense in your pursuit of your legacy.

Over the past two decades, I've spoken to thousands of people in various forms: talks, live streams, masterminds, and one-on-one coaching. These audiences have included people from more than twenty-five countries and all walks of life. Yet they seem to share common frustrations:

- I wish my relationships were more satisfying.
- I feel trapped in my job.
- My life feels overwhelming and I'm tired.
- I wish I had more adventure in my life.
- I want to feel loved.

But underneath all of these frustrations, at a deeper level of the soul, are two questions that I have heard more often than all of the others combined:

- What is my purpose in life?
- How can I feel fully alive?

I've wrestled with all of these questions myself. The pains of my life have been a sober teacher. I've been weak at times, been betrayed, been made bankrupt, lost a spouse, and made many mistakes along my journey. I've also learned that our past does not have to dictate our future. As I'm working to create my own legacy, and helping others discover theirs, I know one thing to be absolutely certain: *We've all been given something great to do and we are the only things holding ourselves back. The beautiful gift of satisfaction you'll experience is to discover your legacy and see it realized!*

There are no exceptions. Every person has been given something to do that will bring them to life and serve others in ways that are beyond anything they could imagine today. In fact, I'll take it one step further. I believe that your legacy has already been written! I'll say it again: we are the ones who have been unknowingly holding it back. I don't need to convince you of this. You intuitively know these two things to be true:

1. There is a magnificent purpose for your life.
2. If you search for it diligently, you'll be shown the way to bring it to life.

This book is here in your hands for one reason: you are already on the path to finding your purpose, and this book will be your guide. You've already begun searching for the deepest and most meaningful things for your life. Be grateful to your own soul for calling you to something great. Celebrate for a moment. You pushed away the noise of this world and made yourself a priority. How many people stay preoccupied with the hectic nature of modern life and never get to asking the deeper questions? Answering these questions adds a richness to everything you experience.

Simply being in the pursuit of your legacy changes the quality of each day. You'll begin to feel the excitement and energy rise up and touch everything you do. I'm grateful to share this journey of discovery with you.

Legacy is a book written to simplify the process and accelerate your pursuit of a life filled with purpose, satisfaction, and impact that your heart is longing for.

The world needs to experience the greatness within you. We need you. We will all benefit when you live out the life you were born to live. This book will help simplify the process and give you the practical daily steps for making it happen.

I want to begin with a story to show you how a legacy was created for a dear friend of mine. Clear your mind and enjoy this story.

Rick's Story of Creating His Legacy

Rick, a salesman in his early forties, felt lost. Daily life was just so, well, daily. Work consumed long hours and pressured him with quotas, deadlines, and details.

He loved his daughter very much, but, as a single dad, he knew he was only giving her the leftovers of his time and energy. But who and what was claiming the best of his time and energy? Were they really more important? Working for a large company meant to him that he was just building someone else's dream. What was his? Did he even have one?

Out of frustration and a crying need in his soul to have something of his own to create, he began writing a book during his breaks and downtimes at work. There is no luxury of waiting for inspiration when you can only capture small windows of time in a day, so he just wrote.

His book took a couple of years to write and finally be ready to share with the world. He asked himself, "Do I want to share this? Was this just for me?" It just felt good to get it out of his soul and into a story that could be shared. Amazingly, the book, *The Safari Adventure Company*, was a success, but not in the way some authors measure. Yes, several thousand copies were sold, but the benefit came when a copy was purchased by a literary professor who saw something deeper in the writing. As an example for her class, she wanted the students to read the book and then have Rick come speak. She arranged to have the university write an invitation letter to pay him to speak to her class—yes, pay him!

Rick couldn't believe it! He could be paid to talk about his book? He spent hours in preparation for his talk. He showed up with excitement to share his passion with them. That talk led to another invitation to speak, and then another. "Why?" he wondered.

Determined to understand, he made it his mission to see whether he could somehow get enough of these invitations to make it into a career! He took courses in public speaking and how to book college speaking gigs, and he networked as best he could. With each talk, he asked for referrals.

In less than one year, he was able to quit his job and more than match his income with college talks. He took it further and crafted a keynote speech he took to corporate retreats and trainings. He was now a professional speaker with time to be at home and be a father to his daughter! It was a dream, and it fueled his life with energy and purpose and fulfillment.

I spoke with his daughter, Rachel, the other day, and she fondly remembered her last days in high school with her dad. As she said it, "Dad had the school admissions number on speed dial so we could go skiing for the day. And we did that often!"

However, in the years that followed, his success started to own him. Yes, he was making more than $300K per year, but he was now on the road so much he began to dislike the very thing that gave him so much fulfillment before. Thinking about how to regain his time, he began to shift his energy to coaching others on how to give talks and become free from their jobs. A year later, "The Speaker Machine" was bringing in more than enough to stay home and coach groups of paying customers. His joy was to see them come to life with new hope and share the messages they were given.

That's when I met Rick. I had married a young woman from Ukraine and blogged about the uniqueness that comes with cross-cultural marriages. On Christmas Day 2010, we spoke for a few hours about a vision he had to create a documentary and have me as its host. We developed a deep friendship and made time to connect almost daily. The documentary never happened, but a following began and I started coaching and teaching on relationships. Over the next three years, I would help him meet his new wife, and beyond that, connect more than two hundred people in marriages across fifteen different countries. In time, that number grew to surpass 450 marriages from more than twenty countries with more than 90 percent still married as of the time of this writing.

I will never forget the time he asked me to talk with one of his Speaker Machine coaching groups as an example of how his system could work to build a new brand. He nearly choked up when he said, "Of everything I've done in my life, I may be the most proud of helping Marcum. Hundreds of new generations have been started, and babies born, because of this work. It's part of my legacy too."

Two days later, he wrote to share with me news about the severe pain he was experiencing because of spurs that had begun growing along his spine. He was a cancer survivor, but this was a new development. He told me how he was pleading with God to give him another decade so he could write a few more books because he saw the good they could do.

He was about to go into radiation treatment when his body became flooded with infection and his system was too weak to overcome it. He passed away on the very day he was to receive the treatment.

I was devastated by the loss of my dear friend. He was only fifty-six years old. I wished he'd had more time as well, but for my own selfish reasons. I loved him.

In the online memorial service, I listened to person after person who spoke so dearly about how Rick had touched their lives, how he'd given them a new direction in life, and memories together they would never forget. He also left a large ranch near Spokane, Washington, to his new wife. But the tearful remembrance from his daughter, Rachel, took all of our hearts.

He did it. He created a beautiful legacy.

You Were Born to Create a Legacy

For most of my life, I thought legacies were only for the rich, the famous, or the inventors of the world. Names like Benjamin Franklin, Theodore Roosevelt, Steve Jobs, and John Wayne came to mind. Rick wouldn't have come to mind, until now.

Rick's life opened my eyes to realize one eternal truth: we are all here to create a legacy—a unique mark on the world that only we can make.

Understanding this shattered all of my excuses:

- You don't need a financial background.
- You don't need to be a numbers whiz.
- You don't need a lot of money.
- You don't need a degree.
- It's never too late to get started.

The Legacy Formula

In the days after Rick's memorial, I thought a lot about what it meant to leave a legacy. I watched the replay of the online memorial service and took notes of what was said about him.

I began my research into creating legacies. I looked up books on the topic but didn't find exactly what I was looking for, which was a formula I could use to create a legacy for myself. But my quest had begun! My next thought was "Who do I know who left an impression on me?" I've known many people who did kind things for me. I remember books that touched me in a profound way or gave me some insights I needed at the time. Is this part of the formula? My curiosity grew.

I started looking at the books that touched on the idea of leaving a legacy. John C. Maxwell, the leadership expert, dedicated a chapter in his book *The 21 Irrefutable Laws of Leadership*, which he titled "The Law of Legacy," so I raced to that chapter to capture his wisdom. There he defined a legacy as what's created when you raise up the next generation of leaders to take your place and continue your work. That may be 100 percent true for leaders in business, but I couldn't relate to it. Is a legacy only what you do in your career? It couldn't be.

I had also heard several authors say, "Think about what you would want people to say at your memorial service, and build your life in that way." The concept seemed solid, especially since my original inspiration was Rick's memorial service. So I ventured out to write my own memorial without success. Have you ever tried such an exercise; to write your own eulogy? It felt awkwardly self-serving. "Here lies Marcum. I remember him well. He was a good guy and had successes in his life." It wasn't as helpful of an idea as I'd hoped.

After exploring several other discussions relating to life and legacy, I came to the working conclusion that:

> *Your legacy is what other people will say about how you touched their lives.*

I felt good about that definition. A legacy isn't something you can say about yourself, nor is it what someone might say to you directly. What someone would say to your face will always be tainted by their desire to impress you in one way or another. *Your legacy is what other people will say about how you touched their lives*, not to you, but as they speak about you with others. I liked it, but I still didn't have a formula for making it happen.

I further asked myself, "Are legacies something acknowledged only after we're gone? Or are there 'living legacies'?" "Of course, there are," I concluded. People can have an amazing legacy while they are still alive, but what is said about them is usually not what they say about themselves. We're blinded on one hand by self-criticism, or by inflated egos on the other. How can we look at ourselves objectively?

I tried to think of an example of a living legacy and Morgan Freeman came to my mind for some reason. OK, what would I say about Morgan Freeman? He makes great movies, has a one-of-a-kind voice, and I feel positive emotions when thinking about him. A few of the parts he played left such an impact on me that I am grateful to him for his performances. But where's the formula I can apply to my hopes for creating a legacy of my own?

I had to let the project go for a while. I didn't seem to be getting any closer to the answer I was looking for. But the burning question was alive in my subconscious. I believe God also heard the cry of my heart for an answer.

Sure enough, in one of those amazing aha moments, I felt the answer come to me: "Study what people are actually saying at memorial services. You will find a pattern there."

I went back through my mind to the memorial service for Rick, as well as the service for my former spouse who passed, and my grandfather. I also reflected on the memorial services of famous people, like Princess Diana, Ronald Reagan, Michael Jackson, and Steve Jobs. The answer must be here somewhere, I thought. To my delight, a pattern did emerge. I was getting excited again!

Here is a snapshot of what I discovered. At memorial services, people talk about one or more of these five categories of the person's legacy:

- People and close relationships
- Experiences shared
- Assets left to heirs
- Creations enjoyed by many
- Expressions of kindness

I pored over these five components—tried rephrasing them—looked for exceptions, but in the end, I couldn't find holes in the formula. If you intentionally invest in each of these five areas of your life, you will create a beautiful legacy!

Wait! Look at the formula! I couldn't believe it. Look at these five components again:

- **P**eople
- **E**xperiences
- **A**ssets
- **C**reations
- **E**xpressions of Kindness

As an acronym, the formula also spelled PEACE! This was it! I knew intuitively that anyone who made even small investments in people, experiences, assets, creations, and expressions of kindness would find a deeply abiding peace and be able to one day leave this earth with peace of mind and a deep sense of satisfaction.

At that moment, I knew I had to share my discovery with you.

In the chapters ahead, you'll learn the *what*, *who*, *how*, and *why* of becoming a legacy maker for yourself. You'll see that the book is divided into four parts:

- Part 1: What's the Truth about Legacies?
- Part 2: Who Are the Legacy Makers?
- Part 3: How to Build Your Legacy—The PEACE Legacy Formula
- Part 4: Why You Should Become a Legacy Maker

Do you feel that inner call to become a legacy maker? Maybe you did, but doubts held you back. Perhaps you previously thought legacies were only for the elite. Maybe you didn't think you were good enough, rich enough, or famous enough to leave a lasting legacy. We're about to change all of that and set you on a path to live with purpose, find fulfillment, and be remembered as you live out your destiny as a legacy maker.

This is going to be the most significant undertaking of your life, and I'm honored to share the journey with you. Let's go!

PART 1

PART 1:

What's the Truth about Legacies?

Before you picked up this book, how would you have defined a legacy? I was astonished by the vast number of definitions I found with a simple Google search.

The definition offered by Google, which it claimed to source from *Oxford Languages,* popped up atop the search results and offered these formal definitions:

1. An amount of money or property left to someone in a will. Example: "My grandmother died and unexpectedly left me a small legacy."
2. An applicant to a particular college or university who is regarded preferentially because a parent or other relative attended the same institution. Example: "Being a legacy increased a student's chance of being accepted to a highly selective college by up to 45 percent."

Are you inspired yet?

Me neither . . .

YourDictionary offered twenty-one different definitions. Among them were:

- Money or property left to someone by a will; bequest.
- Anything handed down from an ancestor.
- A student applying or admitted to a college or university who is a relative of an alumnus.
- A grant by will of personal property or of money.
- The definition of legacy is something that is passed on to you from family, including reputation.
- Being or having to do with something, esp. something outdated or otherwise undesirable, that is carried over from a previous system, business operation, etc.
- Retained under an obsolescent or discarded system, chiefly for purposes of reference.

Then there were the origins in Latin and French . . .

I have to stop there now or sheer boredom will keep you from reading further!

But if you're ever having trouble sleeping, you might find it easier to fall asleep if you spend some time reading through the "official" definitions of legacy . . .

Beyond the boring nature of the definitions, there was nothing clear or concise about them either. No guide to how I could be a legacy maker. None motivated me to want to create anything they were describing.

It was all so contrary to the feeling I had in my gut that your legacy is the by-product of living out your purpose. Your legacy should be the cumulative sum of all the ways you added value to others. Or, as we said in the introduction: ***"Your legacy is what other people will say about how you touched their lives."***

Now that's inspiring!

Better still, this book is your guide to becoming a legacy maker.

And in this first part of the book, I'll share the *truth* about legacies that will not only show you *how* to build a legacy but also inspire you to get started. In these three chapters, I'll

- Help you create your path to meaning and significance
- Give clarity on how to discover your greatness
- Provide applications for being a legacy maker in the four cornerstones of your life

Join me in taking a deeper look into the truth about legacies.

It starts now!

Read on.

Chapter 1:

Legacy: More Than Cars, Cash, and Condominiums

I wish everyone could get rich and famous and have everything they ever dreamed of, so they can see that's not the answer.
—JIM CARREY

They say most millionaires have made it, lost it, and made it again at least once in their lives. Personally, I've built three businesses to more than seven figures in annual revenue, plus a real estate portfolio worth several million dollars. But I also experienced that cycle of complete loss after the crash of 2008, as millions of other people did.

Do you remember how it felt the first time you fell in love? The first time I came into money felt similar, especially after having struggled most of my life prior. Perhaps I felt that way because it was my first time having any sort of wealth, or maybe it felt euphoric because I basically spent it on self-indulgences. As King Solomon said three thousand years ago, "I withheld no pleasure from myself" (Eccles. 2:9–11, Complete Jewish Bible).

Don't let your imagination go too far with that quote, but my lifestyle *was* very opulent compared with my prior years.

I wasn't born into money, so the taste of it was the stuff of dreams. My father was a career pastor. He spent his entire working life serving people and making lower middle-class income. But, in truth, it's not a career you choose for the money. He was and is happy with his choice, and I'm proud of him. Similarly, prior to turning thirty-five, I'd only worked for other people and never earned more than $50K in any given year.

Another reason my first financial success might have felt so euphoric was because I had to fight so hard for it. My wife at the time was a young attorney who was just starting a new law practice. In her second year of business, we decided we also wanted to have a child. It didn't take long to succeed in that effort, and we were elated with the news that we were going to have a child together!

We had dreamed about her taking a few years off from work to dedicate to this new little one before returning to it. However, looking at our finances, there was no way we could afford for her to take so much time off; it would cut our income in half! Not only would we be expanding our little family, but we had just bought a house and needed her income to afford the mortgage.

I quickly realized that if she stayed home when this child was born, I'd need to double my income in the next eight months! I'd never earned that much money before, and I had no idea how to make it happen now.

I quickly started shifting back and forth between focused intensity and panic. I was desperate to think of ways to double my income in eight months. I dove deep into studying leadership and business planning. I explored ideas for businesses I could start. I asked everyone I knew for ideas and anyone they could introduce me to who might be able to help.

A college friend had an idea for a fuzzy logic search engine, so I wrote a business plan to approach angel investors, but we clashed on parts of it and went our separate ways. My dad introduced me to a venture capital attorney, Mario Rosati, who helped get me going on another business idea.

More on that in chapter 2. I never did get the plan in a final form, but I impressed several Silicon Valley executives with my passion and creativity and ended up with an offer to be an exclusive distributor to California for a growing publicly traded company. In less than eight months, I'd made more money than we needed! The saying that "Necessity is the mother of invention" was so true! I found entrepreneurship to be an adrenaline-filled ride that was intoxicating and immensely rewarding.

Things kept getting better and better. By the early 2000s, I was making more money than I'd ever *seen* before. I grew that distributorship to $5.5 million in sales and was able to upgrade our home to a 5,500-square-foot house that had been the model home for a new housing development. It was two doors down from a forty-seven-acre park in a new suburb of Natomas Park in Sacramento, California. Even better, the system I had put into place made the business run on autopilot.

I started spending a lot of the money on myself. I traveled to Brazil, Costa Rica, and the northern regions of Saskatchewan, Canada, for exotic fishing expeditions with members of the board of directors for the company I was representing. I drove a Mercedes convertible and had a luxury Jaguar as our family car. I took guitar lessons and learned how to record music. I also owned seven investment properties that were doubling in value and all producing positive cash flow.

Unfortunately, money doesn't shield you from all of life's pains. My wife developed a debilitating disorder and ended up passing away, leaving me a single dad with a young son. A few years later, however, I married again, which gave me renewed hope and optimism for the future.

Shortly after that, the crash of 2008 wiped me out. As you know from history, the global financial markets collapsed almost overnight. Businesses and entire industries were devastated. Home values dropped by half or more in some places. Millions of people lost their jobs, investments, and savings.

I was no different. When the value of my rental properties got cut in half, I quickly ended up financially underwater. On top of that, my industry was crushed, and the publicly traded company I was working with collapsed, causing my income to disappear completely. With no income and the values of my properties cut in half, I was financially done in a little more than one year's time. The banks took the houses and cars. I had to move my family into a small condo in Anaheim, California, that my parents weren't using.

Although I'd been a generally optimistic person most of my life, you might imagine that all of this had a heavy impact. My ego was wrapped up in my ability to support my family. I had to swallow my pride and move my family into my parents' condo, with no income at all.

All the admiration I had received for being a successful person was gone. I used to smile with pride from the daily compliments and admiration I received on my cars, home, or exotic travel stories.

On Christmas Day 2010, we found ourselves living in a condo that was basically a shrine to Disneyland and Disney decor. My parents had been season pass holders to the parks and covered every wall with trinkets and souvenirs with mouse ears. I was grateful that we had a place to live, although to this day, it's hard not to think about living in that condo whenever I see a pair of mouse ears.

I know my story is not unique. Millions of people were displaced and financially ruined in the crash of '08. Many businesses, and jobs, were erased. But I naively hoped it wouldn't affect me. I hung on as long as I could. But, by the end of 2010, there was nothing left that I could do. And, although I wouldn't choose to go through it again, if not for my experience making so much money only to lose it, I might never have discovered the PEACE Legacy Formula. Had I not tasted superficial success and then lost it from 2008 to 2010, you might not be holding this book.

The Legacy System

Although the Legacy system you'll learn in this book would not be documented until years later, I can look back through the lens of the legacy system, with the benefit of hindsight, and take inventory of exactly where I was in 2010:

- **People**: I went from having a thriving circle of friends to just my wife, son, and a new friend named Rick. I felt alone.
- **Experiences**: I went from exotic travel and adventures to watching how much gas I was using in the car to save money. I felt bored and bankrupt.
- **Assets**: I went from being a millionaire with a business generating $5.5 million per year to hoping the checking account wouldn't be overdrawn. I lived with stress and nervous tension.
- **Creations**: The handful of songs I'd recorded were never published. There was nothing I had created that could reach people I hadn't met or that would outlive me.
- **Expressions of Kindness**: I'd have to go back to the days of my involvement with men's groups in church to find the last time I added enough value to someone outside of my family that they would thank me for my role in their lives. At that point, I was making no contributions to the world around me.

I think back to that life of being self-absorbed and almost completely devoid of people, experiences, assets, creations, and expressions of kindness. After the financial loss, I felt like I was nothing. All I had was my family, which isn't nothing, but I felt even worse when my wife had to go to work waiting tables so we could pay our bills.

My entire identity had been built around my financial success, and it was gone. But I will give my wife at the time the credit for her words of wisdom as she reassured me, "Babe, money will come and go, but we have each other. That's what really matters." Her words provided some comfort and perspective.

A New Opportunity

Although that time was full of pain, it was not without opportunity. For me, my new opportunity came when I was given an office on the lot at Paramount Studios by a friend who ran an independent film company. He hired me to write business plans, or "treatments" as they call them, for independent film projects. I enjoyed the work but made only about $500 per plan, and they didn't come often enough to support a family.

It was at this time, however, that Rick came into our lives. He'd seen a video I made when I was doing well and talking about my relationship with my Ukrainian wife. Something about the video resonated with him, and he encouraged me to start an online coaching business. His radiant energy was contagious and very welcome. I started a weekly broadcast with him, and we grew a following. Although there wasn't a lot of money in this business yet, it was a powerful antidote to my self-flagellation. The men I was helping were truly grateful for the help and making strides in their own development and confidence. My audience continued growing.

As part of my coaching, I conducted weekly live broadcasts, one of which happened to land on my fiftieth birthday in 2013. I'll never forget it. I set up my laptop next to the firepit on my back porch, lit a cigar, enjoyed a glass of wine, and made some great connections with these brothers online.

When I joined the broadcast, instead of my typical teaching, I simply asked the men whether they wouldn't mind sharing any ways I'd helped make a difference in any of their lives. Frankly, I needed encouragement in that moment and humbled myself enough to ask for it.

These men delivered in a beautiful way. For the next hour, one after another chimed in to let me know how much they had grown. Their relationships were better. They were more fulfilled in life. Their incomes had grown. One man gained the discipline to get in shape and lose one hundred pounds. Another had started a side hustle that had become a growing business. Others talked about finding the courage to go back to school in pursuit of a new dream. Another began saying yes to wild adventures that changed his life. The stories continued even after the broadcast as one after another posted comments on my website about their stories of change.

I was overwhelmed, humbled, and so grateful. I'd never felt that way in all of my days of affluence. I'd never really touched another person in such profound ways as I had done with these men. I had no idea what the feeling was but, whatever it was, I didn't want to ever let it go. It grabbed me and changed me forever.

I spent the next several years helping thousands more before expanding my efforts into philanthropic work with orphanages in Ukraine, which would truly become one of the hallmarks of my living legacy.

The lesson I learned was clear: a true legacy is one that touches others in a positive way.

The power of the PEACE Legacy Formula I share in this book is how simple it is. In fact, it's surprisingly simple to create your own legacy. And you can do so by doing the things you were born to do, touching people only you can touch, and creating amazing things you were meant to create.

And you can do all of this while living a life you will love. I found tremendous joy and meaning that had nothing to do with money. Best of all, when I did start to build a financial base again, I did so as a changed man.

I would go on to build two other seven-figure businesses, but the experience with those was dramatically different. I was truly connected to my heart. I found a deeper sense of satisfaction. I was inspired with a higher purpose. Although I wouldn't choose to experience the weight of such loss again, the lessons I learned have helped me build something much more valuable and personally rewarding. I want this for you too.

In the world of great quotes, I wanted to be among the first authors to attribute a bit of wisdom that came originally from an AI, Grok, the AI from X…

 Not all heroes wear capes, but they do make the world a better place.—Grok[1]

1 Sir Doge of the Coin (@dogeofficialceo) "I ask Grok for the good news every day." X, Dec 11, 2023, 9:56 AM, https://x.com/dogeofficialceo/status/1734225719008317566?s=51

I used to think a legacy was all about wealth and power. But there will always be someone with more money and power. I used to think that a legacy was about creating a public image of success and accolades from fame. Now I know that can all be taken away. Measuring our success based on wealth, power, or public image is a sad game that can never be won and, ultimately, brings no lasting satisfaction.

I learned that legacy is measured by the value we can transfer to others. I also learned about the great power we have in our choices. We can choose who we want to benefit from our good favor. We can choose who we also ignore. If you've ever been involved in social media work, you know exactly what I'm talking about. And we can choose the things in life we decide have value. If we decide to build a legacy, we must first have things of value within us that we can transfer to others. It means we must have an open heart that truly wants to see others become better because we were here. It means we get to decide what's important to us and lead a life that can help others do the same in their lives.

These core values are part of a winning game that brings deep satisfaction that builds a life that will be remembered fondly for years to come.

This is legacy.

It's a new way to live.

It's about a life of service.

It's about turning darkness into light.

It's about being aware of the needs around us.

It's about living with purpose.

It's about being mission-driven.

It's an energy and passion that wakes you up every morning.

It's about going to bed each night with peace of mind and a smile on your face.

And all of this will be yours, made with intention, from what you'll learn in the pages that follow.

What I'm offering is a simple formula to bring this to life for you and for as many of our fellow human beings as possible. It is literally a formula for PEACE.

Through it, you can live each day with peace and finish your life at peace with yourself and the world.

Just imagine a world filled with people striving to build this type of legacy. It would change everything. Greed would be replaced with intentions to serve. Selfish people would become selfless. Ego-driven people would become humble and giving. The list goes on.

Whether you've already created many successes in your life, or you are rebuilding, as I was, or you are just getting started on your life journey for the first time, you can start building a legacy you'll be proud of the very day you start following the PEACE Legacy Formula I share in this book.

In the next chapter, you'll learn the principle of compounding and creating greatness and how that helps you build a legacy. If that seems "big" or intimidating, don't worry. Like the entire PEACE Legacy Formula, it's refreshingly simple.

The truth is, greatness has always been in you. It's in you right now. You may have just needed to get out of your own way or tweak some of your daily habits to set it free. But greatness will come if you follow what you'll learn.

It's your turn to be great.

And now is the time to begin.

Chapter 2:

Using Legacy to Achieve True, Enduring Greatness

Everybody can be great—because anybody can serve.
—MARTIN LUTHOR KING JR.

T he very idea of being a legacy maker is inspirational to me, and most people, if they'll listen to the calling of their hearts. The thought that we can live with purpose and impact and be remembered is deep in every soul. It's our nature to want to know we made a difference in people's lives and made the world better for having been here. Even more, to make sure that our time here on earth won't be forgotten.

What legacies look like will vary from person to person, of course. Some people focus almost entirely on their family and friends during their lifetime. Those people typically don't have the desire to expand their efforts beyond their immediate circles because they find it deeply satisfying, as some parents find with raising successful children. There's nothing wrong with that. And, in reality, the impact these people make in their immediate circles will create ripples far beyond their family and friends over time. John C. Maxwell notably said, "True success is when those who know you the best, love you the most." Reread that a few times. There is tremendous wisdom in these words.

Other people want to impact larger circles during their lifetime by making a difference in their communities and the world around them, in addition to their close circles. I happen to fall into this category, having developed a deep desire to positively impact people I don't know and might never know, in addition to my family, friends, and colleagues in business. That desire is part of what led me to do philanthropic work with my nonprofit, Abundance International, and to write this book. We've been bringing life-giving aid to orphans in Ukraine since 2012 and loving every aspect of it. And I believe this book can change millions of lives over time.

Many people feel a deep calling to impact the world but don't yet have the confidence to move forward with a plan of action. Of course, throughout the book, I'm going to share how anyone can make a positive impact on the world no matter where you are or what small or great resources you may have today.

People's visions for their legacies aren't static either. Some people might start by focusing on the broader world and realize their deeper desire is to focus on changing their family tree.

Others might start out focused mostly on their family and friends and develop a desire to make an even broader impact over time. In fact, a great way to change the world is to start by first changing yourself and making a positive impact on your friends and family by being the example of the change you want to see in the world.

When you focus on changing yourself first so you can make an impact on your family, then your family and you can make an impact on your community. You and your community can impact your country. And by focusing on yourself and creating ripples throughout your family, community, and country, you can eventually change the world.

Whatever your vision is for your legacy, the result remains the same: your legacy can help you achieve true, enduring greatness far beyond your years on earth. And in this chapter, I'll share exactly how to begin doing just that.

Fueling the Legacy Makers

It all begins when we acknowledge that our core desire is to be a legacy maker. Legacy makers are the people who take action, who spend their days living out the PEACE formula for legacy creation. Their natural thoughts, desires, and actions build their legacies as an outpouring of their hearts. I'll talk deeper about that concept throughout the book; however, before we get into that, I want to first talk about "fuel."

Legacy makers are sometimes others-focused to a fault, sacrificing themselves for the sake of others. To them, knowing they are impacting others positively is enough for them to take service to an extreme, living in poverty because they want to focus every penny on a cause bigger than themselves. Others make self-care a priority so they can best serve others from an abundance of energy. The idea is that we can do more good in the world when we've also taken care of ourselves.

One challenge legacy makers sometimes face, however, is physical and emotional fuel. Some legacy makers can become so focused on their bigger goals that they don't take the time to celebrate the impact they are making along the way. Overwhelm and exhaustion can take them out of the game if they're not careful.

That's why it's so important to approach legacy making with a mindset that you will have a lot to celebrate along the way, even before you've made an impact on a single person. At all times, remember that building a legacy is a journey on which you embark for the rest of your life. It is not a destination you reach one time and check a box that you've created your legacy. True legacy makers will continue to grow their impact, working deeper into people's lives or broader to directly reach even more people's lives for as long as they are able.

Thus, if you're waiting for one big event to tell you that you've achieved a goal, you might be waiting a long time. But if you look at all the little things you're doing to make an impact on yourself and others along the way, you'll find things to celebrate in abundance.

So celebrate the little steps you take on your journey. Be proud of yourself for making the commitment to build a legacy and take a moment to congratulate yourself for declaring that you are a true legacy maker— because the moment you make that declaration, you are.

The little moments along your journey will fuel you. They will push you through obstacles. They will remind you of why it is that you are working so hard to impact the world. To legacy makers, there is nothing like the feeling of receiving messages from people who just want to thank you for helping them in one way or another.

Perhaps you've already received messages like those in your life. Maybe you've helped someone get through a difficult situation or inspired them to launch a business they always dreamed of. Maybe the example you set by being so passionate and determined will motivate someone to break through their excuses and finally get on the path toward whatever they had been dreaming of. Most people know what they are supposed to be doing, or that next step that they've been putting off. You may be the one who gets them to stop thinking and start doing, and they will make their contribution to the world.

Although you and I have likely not yet met, if you're a legacy maker at heart, I'm willing to bet you've positively impacted a number of people already. And I hope I do get to meet you, or that you'll write to me, so I can hear all about it.

It's amazing to think about how many people you can encourage in your lifetime and what they will go on to do because of you. They will go on to touch others you may never meet or even know about. You just pushed the first domino in a chain that goes on beyond your imagination. Perhaps one of the people you touch becomes the next Nobel Prize winner, inventor, or creator of a charity that changes the world.

Don't underestimate the importance of everyone you come in contact with. It's incredible to see how little encouragement people need to believe they really can make a difference.

The beauty of building that kind of legacy is it only takes three things. In fact, every person who has created a great legacy has had these three things in common. Whether it was Steve Jobs, Maya Angelou, Jeff Bezos, or the teacher of the year, they've all worked through these three stages:

- They started.
- They worked based on their values.
- They kept going.

That's it. And although it might seem oversimplified, the truth is everything else involved is "just details." What each of these people started and the specific values that directed their work might be different, but they all started, worked based on their values, and kept going.

You'll find those three simple things in every single person who has achieved greatness.

And if you want to achieve greatness and build a legacy you can be proud of, you can begin building that legacy by doing exactly that too. Here's how.

Start

Starting is certainly the most underrated secret to success, and it's seldom discussed. Yet, it's the equivalent of opening the magic genie's bottle when it comes to building a legacy. It uncorks the power of limitless opportunity, drive, and ambition.

Ignore this at your own peril. The very act of starting unleashes a power that shouldn't be taken for granted; it fuels you from within. And treating the concept of starting as less important than any other step in your journey is a recipe for failure.

In short, you need to start with great intention as a commitment to yourself and the world you wish to impact. Starting is a big deal.

But the enemy of action is procrastination. It's so seductive. You may even feel like you've started just by thinking about your dreams or making your plans. While thinking and planning are helpful and necessary, there is no substitute for doing the work and taking the steps necessary on your journey. And the first step is the most important.

One of my more broadly known quotes is this: "You can't steer a parked car."

What I have found so common in my coaching programs was people who seemed to be stuck in perpetual planning mode. They write out their plans, goals, mission statements, and sometimes even pick a brand name for their venture. But none of those, although important, bring with them the power that doing the work does. Let me explain.

The ancient Greeks believed that we all have a set of inner warriors who will rise up within to empower us to fight our battles when called upon. I'm sure you've felt them come to life at times. Maybe you had an idea for a new business venture and wrestled through all of the thoughts about what it could look like. But something thrilling happens to your energy level when you take the first real step of action. You may have put down the deposit on a vendor or pitched the concept to the first prospective investor. It's thrilling! But why?

How is making a real pitch different from thinking about it when you conceptualize the project? Theoretically, it should be more exciting to plan something than make a presentation. My conclusion for why that's not the case is that your inner warriors don't need to engage in planning. They're only needed when it's time to take action. When you have to get up the nerve to put your money into something, make the calls to recruit people, or walk the streets promoting, you generate an internal excitement that turns into power because you are actually doing the work!

Imagine for a moment that your inner warriors are sitting next to you while you're planning the impact you want to make. You're thinking. You're probably writing some things down. Maybe you're answering questions I've proposed in sections of this book.

What are the warriors doing? Nothing. They're just sitting next to you. There's nothing for them to do. But the second you take your first step forward, they jump out of their chairs and declare, "Let's go! We're actually going to do this!" You feel their energy. They bring a level of excitement and boldness. They think constantly of other ways you could do it even better and faster.

Often, people go through planning phases and quit because they don't "feel it." They begin to doubt themselves or think they won't have what it will take to get the job done. But that's almost always because they haven't awakened the inner warriors who are waiting to help make it happen. They feel a lack of enthusiasm.

In that state of planning, the project may feel flat, especially for those who are detail oriented and don't want to start until every risk is mitigated and success is guaranteed. But this just leads to more procrastination and more excuses for why it isn't time to get started yet. And many times, those doubts and fears simply grow and kill the whole project before it gets off the ground.

It's a shame to think about how many legacies were never built because they were never started. Starting matters.

What have you got to lose if you take action? What's the worst-case scenario? That you discover what you had thought you wanted to do isn't what you actually want to do? That you need different resources or skills to do what you want to do? That you realize you "can't" do what you wanted to do exactly how you had thought it would play out? Then what? You adjust, refocus, and start again.

Now compare that to the best-case scenario. The best-case scenario is that it works and inspires even more. Action attracts people to projects. As Theodore Roosevelt proclaimed in his now famous "Man in the Arena" speech from 1910, "It is not the critic who counts, . . . The credit belongs to the man who is actually in the arena," who counts. When people see you in the arena doing the work, and loving what you're doing, they will ask whether they can join you. They can "smell the smoke of battle" on you. You won't get that from someone watching you typing plans on your computer. Get in the arena. Get started.

It doesn't matter if you've started and stumbled countless times before. I did. Had I quit after my 2010 bankruptcy and resigned myself to punching a time clock for the rest of my working years, I would never have built Abundance International. I would never have helped all those orphans in Ukraine achieve a better life. And I would never have helped people in my coaching programs build better lives for themselves. This book would have never come to life.

So, if you've started and stumbled, start again. Never underestimate the power of starting again either. As Dorothea Brande said, "Act boldly and unseen forces will come to your aid."

Once you start taking even the first action steps toward one of your legacy projects or goals, you'll feel the power of your inner warriors rise up and your excitement will build. Look for this energy. Cherish it. You can live in this power every day because, as I will discuss later, you can take steps every day to make your legacy a reality. Once you learn to live in this energy, you'll never want to experience another day without it. Action is the stuff of life. Just start and then stay in motion!

Values-Driven

If you could put one declaration behind all of your legacy projects, it should be the simple statement "This is important to me."

It doesn't matter what legacy you are looking to build. It just matters that it's important to you. If it's important to you, all you need to do is start, stay true to the values upon which your legacy goal is based, and keep going.

If you're unsure what values you want to pursue by building your legacy, don't worry. A lot of people who are just beginning their journeys as legacy makers haven't sat down and thought through their values in detail. At its most basic level, your values are simply what's important to you. If you want to take it a step further, all you need to do for now is to ask yourself what is important to you that others can benefit from. If that's all you think about now when it comes to values, you'll be fine. In part 3 of this book, we'll take a deep dive into all five aspects of the PEACE Legacy Formula. That discussion will help add clarity and confidence into what is most important to you and why.

But know this, if something isn't important to you, you won't finish it. And if it's of vital importance to you, you can't *not* do it.

And that's what separates the legacy makers from others. Legacy makers spend much of their lives pursuing things that are so important to them that they can't *not* pursue them. And as they achieve more, they continue to explore what's most important to them at the next stage and why. These values consume everything they do—from the causes they champion to the people they spend time with. If something is not consistent with their values, they intentionally make no time for it.

But where do these "values" come from? In the case of many successful ventures, they are often born out of frustration and the conviction that there must be a better way to do something. When an entrepreneur feels that they have a unique solution to something that really irks them, they become driven to prove it to—and share it with—the world! When someone discovers a message that changes their lives and they believe they can help others too, they are driven to make it happen.

Thus, at its core, begin exploring your values by asking yourself the following questions:

- What is important to me today?
- If I could share one message with the world, what would it be?
- What problem do I wish someone could solve that would make a meaningful difference in my daily life?
- What frustrates me on a regular basis?

Your *immediate* answers to those questions will start to reveal what's important enough to you to get you to take action and do the hard work that it takes to solve meaningful problems.

When I've hosted mastermind groups and asked members to share what they think the problems of the world are, the answers range. One felt that getting clean water to places that don't have it is critical for saving millions of lives. Another talked about how clear-cutting the rainforests is reducing the green footprint in the world and that trees are the source of the air we breathe. And as you know, my heart is for supporting orphans in emerging economies, such as Ukraine, where I've focused my efforts to date.

Some people still struggle to identify values based on those questions, seeing them as "big" questions to identify one message or a problem to solve. I typically work with those people to identify what they are already doing and explore what their current activities suggest is important to them. If that sounds like you, ask yourself these two questions:

1. Are there recurring themes to what I post on social media?
2. What causes do I support by volunteering my time or donating money?

The interesting thing to me is to see just how many people do nothing about their frustrations other than share posts on their Facebook page. They might believe that venting frustrations online might win some argument or make some passive-aggressive point to someone they hope will see their post. To some of them, they think they did something meaningful by the act of posting a meme. Others post as if they believe that their one issue should be everyone else's cause too, but are they actually doing anything substantive to solve the problem?

The same is true about our time and money. Where do we spend our time and money? With many people's schedules and finances so tight, examining where we are spending the limited resources we have can be very revealing.

Finally, don't compare your dream to anyone else's dream. It doesn't have to save the universe from alien invaders. Your heart may yearn to give love and attention to the seniors in your local care home. Your passion was given to you for a reason: you were meant to be part of the solution.

The world has many problems to solve. If everyone felt strongly about the same cause, the world would be left with countless problems that never got any attention.

If your heart is captured by the need for clean water in emerging economies, start work on a new way to get it done, or join forces with others who already are. If you clearly see how a product or system could be made better, then look into how it could be accomplished. You're probably not the only one frustrated by these things. What would be required in terms of development, investment, and market adoption?

Follow your frustrations! They may lead to a huge calling. And it will be *your* calling and part of *your* legacy.

On the other side of values-driven ventures are those born from creative inspiration. Perhaps you've been to a Broadway show, visited an art gallery, or attended a concert, and an inspiration hit you for an artistic project you feel would inspire the world.

Positive inspiration is truly a gift from deep within your spirit. In fact, the word "inspire" comes from combining the words "in spirit." We are all called to be creators, for we are made in the image of the Creator. I hope you've experienced some form of creative inspiration in your life. There is nothing like it. Your entire being glows with an energy and excitement to bring something to life from deep within you.

Please understand this: even passions born out of frustration will switch to positive and creative energy once you start to work on the solution—*your* solution to the problem. It will be something so important to you that you must see it come to life. Now you're living from your values.

This is how legacy makers create. They are values-driven. And they spend their days pursuing things that are important to them, from frustration, passion, creative inspiration, or otherwise.

Keep Going

Ultimately, no one escapes the monotony inherent in simply doing the work. Glowing emotions may fade into the difficult tasks accompanied by birthing a vision. There will be days when you just do the work because it must be done. Nothing glamorous. You often work alone. Some of the details of the vision won't work, and new systems must be created; sometimes requiring a complete restart.

That's why it's so important to pursue something important to *you*. Otherwise, you won't get out of bed when it's cold or get behind the computer when you're not "feeling it." Your dedication to your passion is the solution to the monotony in doing the work.

Look no further than Steve Jobs for a great example of how passion and doing the work can tie into incredible things. He once told an audience that most of the products Apple was producing were imagined before the technologies for making them had even been invented. He said, "You can't connect the dots looking forward; you can only connect them looking backwards. So you have to trust that the dots will somehow connect in your future."

In other words, just get started on your vision in faith that everything you need will come from the effort. If it's important to you, you'll push through the uncertainty and figure out the details along the way. As I said earlier, you can't steer a parked car. But once in motion, you can adjust with the twists and turns along the way.

All legacy makers, and other great achievers, have had to fight through incremental setbacks, overcome the drudgery of the work, and combat their own doubts in order to achieve their goals. But they kept going, sometimes on faith that the answers would come, and other times simply because they couldn't *not* keep going toward a goal about which they were so passionate.

I have seen both sides of this. There was a time in 1998 when I was offered to have my idea for a business presented to angel investors by Mario Rosati, cofounder of Wilson Sonsini Goodrich & Rosati, what I understood to be the largest Silicon Valley venture capital law firm at that time. All I had to do was get him a completed business plan.

In those days, crazy things were getting funded. I had three veteran advisors working with me to flesh out the concepts and critique my business plan. The short story was that one of the three didn't see the vision because he thought it could easily be copied by a larger competitor. I was in my early thirties and these men were giants to me. I caved to this one man's opinion and stopped. In hindsight, I just needed to keep going and get a plan—any plan—into Mr. Rosati's hands and we would have found the investors because they would have trusted *his* endorsement of my idea. Instead, I stopped.

Thinking back, I wonder what would have happened had I kept going. What would have been the worst-case scenario if I'd still pushed forward even though one of the three didn't believe in what I was doing? Perhaps I still wouldn't have been funded. On the other hand, maybe I would have found the sources of funding with Mario's help. Simply by completing the task, I would have learned how to create a world-class business plan and how to present to high-level angel investors. The experience alone would have been worth the effort. Either way, at least I'd have had no regrets because I persevered to the very end.

I don't want this to ever be your story. In chapter 9, Assets, I'll tell you more about how to evaluate your business or start-up, create your business plan and pitch deck, and even be presented to investors if all of the elements are in place. I wish I'd had this help when I had my opportunity. Be determined to accept no excuses and live with no regrets. Persevere.

All great achievers and legacy makers start, are values-driven, *and keep going*. There are no exceptions to this. If I'd understood this in my early thirties, I'm sure I would have been one of those Silicon Valley start-ups you'd have heard about. But I stopped. I want this book to help you avoid the mistakes I've made and seen. Your greatness awaits.

Think Bigger

Now that you have the fuel and drive, it's time to think big—really big. Imagine a scenario where your efforts have been rewarded with big breaks. You've met world-changers who could get you on world stages of influence and success. Imagine you've got that multimillion-dollar investment. Imagine being featured on magazine covers for the greatness you've created. Imagine that this is your life now. Feel it. Breath it. See it clearly. It's not overwhelming. It's you. You got there by creating value and doing the work. You earned it. How big could you go? Creating greatness should be, well, great.

I know I've talked a lot about creating legacies for anyone, and I believe it deeply from the core of my being. Anne Sullivan only had to invest herself in one person, Helen Keller, to make an impact heard around the world one hundred years later. But I also know that we often sell ourselves short with self-imposed limitations. Your creator is not limited, and he can do bigger things with and through you than you can imagine now. Can you dream God-sized dreams? Have you asked him what he dreamed for you when he created you? It often feels like the world is holding us back, but we shouldn't be helping it. Only you and your maker know what possibilities your future may hold.

Dream bigger. Your greatness may be lying dormant within you. It's time to bring it to life!

Chapter 3:

The Four Cornerstones of Legacy That Legacy Makers Develop

The two most important days in your life are
the day you are born and the day you find out why.
—MARK TWAIN

By the time I turned thirty, I felt I was progressing well in life. I had a family I loved and enjoyed spending time with. I had a good job in commercial printing sales that I'd done for several years and knew very well. I was an active community leader in men's small groups and found great satisfaction in this fellowship of men. By age thirty-eight, I'd started my first business and it was growing rapidly. I took some of the money I was making and invested in rental properties. I thought I had it all figured out and was building something bigger than myself.

But when the crash of 2008 came, it wiped out my business, took my properties, and I found myself living in a new city with just my family, as I mentioned in chapter 1. I had no community connection or friends anywhere nearby.

I learned the hard way that what I thought was a budding legacy was built on a faulty foundation. I'd narrowed my focus to things that were subject to economic conditions beyond my control and not based on service. As a result, my legacy plan was far too fragile. I needed a legacy plan with enough diversification that a loss in any single area would not take out the entire plan. I needed for there to be many more aspects to replace losses in any one area and investments in people that would survive setbacks. So I began to look for more ways to apply myself and grow. I also expanded my awareness of the additional ways I could become part of things bigger than myself.

As I began to learn about others who had built lasting legacies, I realized they always built on more than one of the key areas of their life. They didn't have just one quality relationship; they had a network of people who supported them and touched their world in different ways. They didn't have just one source of income, leaving everything they needed subject to the whims of one job or company. They built multiple sources of income so, even if they were subject to layoffs or downsizing, they weren't completely crushed. They built side hustles and other streams of income. People who built lasting legacies also didn't just show expressions of kindness to immediate friends and family; they understood that every person they encountered could be better for having met them if they expressed kindness.

In business, I learned that legacy makers were proactive, never relying on past successes or methods to lead them in the future. Instead, they constantly improved products, services, and systems while adding additional revenue opportunities to sell to new and existing customers.

These lessons have stuck with me for years. For example, a travel business I built in Ukraine died when the war hit in early 2022. Had I relied on that one business, as I had in my late thirties and early forties, I would have been crushed again. The orphanages we were supporting through my nonprofit, Abundance International, would also have suffered greatly, as they would have lost the financial backing that was made possible by the travel business. However, because I had built Abundance International as a formal not-for-profit corporation years earlier, people all around the world were able to easily donate funds to support our efforts.

We were in a position to receive donations when the invasion happened. That event redirected my energies and focus to expanding Abundance International's outreach, going from supporting two orphanages to more than twenty in a matter of months.

This time, when disaster struck, all of my eggs were not in one basket. Diversification more than helped me fill the gap created by the loss of one business, and it gave me something even greater to do. I'm also passionately working to put all of this experience together to support you on your quest to become a legacy maker. Please visit MarcumDavis.com and join the legacy maker movement.

Most importantly, I didn't have to scramble from total loss to throw something together to keep the bills paid. I had learned my lesson and prepared ahead of time, so they were already in place when disaster struck.

This was critical because it can take time for ventures to start generating revenue. It took more than a year to gain approval for our 501(c)(3) nonprofit status with the IRS, but I'd completed the process many years before. Had I waited until the invasion to seek 501(c)(3) nonprofit status, I never would have been able to raise enough money that ended up being so critical for all of those children.

I also had shifted how I connected with people in every area of my life, so those connections would continue with me no matter what I did next. Additionally, I'd spent a year before the war developing a fitness app and line of supplements called Authentic Strength, which I'll tell you more about in chapter 6, as a way to help a different group of people and further diversify.

I can't even imagine the personal disaster that would have hit me if I hadn't built the shelter before the storm. I learned the lessons of the '00s, when we got comfortable and thought the glory days of that economy would go on forever. Millions of us were blindsided by the crash of 2008. But I hate to ask the question "How many of those millions of people took steps to avoid being hit when the pandemic pounded us all?" I don't know how many of those people were prepared, but I'm confident the legacy makers were.

Preparing for the Cycles

Everything is cyclical. As I write these words, the world is experiencing high inflation, rising interest rates, and a slowing economy. But just a few years earlier, inflation was virtually nonexistent, interest rates were low, and the economy was strong. And while I don't position myself as an economic fortune teller, history tells us that there will be good times ahead, followed by challenging times, and good times again. I'd love to be able to tell you exactly when those shifts will happen or what they will look like. I can't. But I promise you they are coming, just like the seasons of the year. And the people who are intentional about preparing for the downturns during the upcycles find the downturns to be more of an inconvenience than a catastrophe.

So it's even more important to make hay while the sun shines and fill your barns before winter. As they said in *Game of Thrones*, winter is coming. But that is true of all of the seasons of life.

Cycles don't just apply to economic ups and downs. Every part of our lives will cycle. Our relationships will have ups and downs. Our physical health will have ups and downs. And our mental health will as well. Our challenge is to learn to love our lives no matter where we are in the cycles; no matter what the "weather" of uncontrollable circumstances brings. Life, while not perfect, is beautiful. And if you do it right, you'll be able to enjoy yourself sitting by your fireplace with a good cup of coffee in peace when the next storms come. Know that the storms are a sign that good times are right around the corner as well. If you've prepared, you will be the "calm in the storm" for all of those around you.

Becoming a legacy maker shifts your entire awareness of how you approach every aspect of your life. You approach people, experiences, and accomplishments from a bigger perspective—one of lasting impact, connection, and joy. You begin to naturally see ways to incorporate your legacy plan into your personal life, career, community engagements, and business in ways that will add richness to your daily experiences and attract other big-thinkers into your life.

And you'll prepare for the downturns during the good times to make sure you can continue to make a positive impact on the world no matter what.

Finding PEACE in the Four Cornerstones: Personal, Career, Community, and Business

Over the years, I've talked with many people about the legacies they were building. Throughout those conversations, a pattern seemed to emerge: even some of the most intentional legacy makers had achieved some level of PEACE in one or two areas of their lives but rarely had anyone achieved the full PEACE formula in all four cornerstone areas:

1. Personal
2. Career
3. Community
4. Business

Some had achieved PEACE in their personal lives, with strong relationships, memorable experiences, significant assets, creations that would outlast their time on earth, and regular expressions of kindness that people will remember for years to come. But many of those people struggled in their careers (working a job they despised), community (having few connections beyond family and a small circle of friends), or business (still living with their "dream business" trapped inside them).

Others had achieved PEACE in their careers to the detriment of their personal lives (spending little time and building few connections with friends and family), community (having no connections beyond their business network), or even businesses (still performing tasks that should be delegated, outsourced, or eliminated if they want to do their highest and best work).

Still others had achieved PEACE in their communities or careers but struggled in their personal or business lives.

The pattern was clear: most people seemed to progress in one, or at most two, cornerstone areas of their lives but struggled greatly in the other two or three.

If that feels like you, don't fret. In fact, I'd humbly suggest you might celebrate. If you can achieve PEACE in one or two areas of your life, there's no reason you can't do the same in the other cornerstone areas. There's no reason you can't build relationships with people on a personal level and not do the same in your community, career, or business. Relationships are relationships. Likewise, there's no reason you could create memorable experiences in the workplace but not with your family or community.

Regarding your business, I would counsel every executive and entrepreneur to be the legacy maker for their company. Your company deserves to have a legacy plan in place to communicate your values. A corporate legacy plan transforms a business into something great and lasting. Passing along the core values that make it great to the next generation doesn't happen by default. I love talking with companies about their corporate legacy. Applying the PEACE Legacy Formula to your business should be even more important than your vision and mission statements because it creates something tangible for your people and customers to grasp. More than formulaic mission statements, your corporate legacy ensures the company will live on and not lose its identity and culture.

The reason I created separate categories for career and business is because that's how I see them. Your career is how you conduct yourself in your work environment. Your business is its own entity and needs to create its own legacy. I hope that makes sense to you.

If you can achieve PEACE in one area, you can do the same in the others. All you need to do is start, be driven by your values, and keep going.

For the rest of this book, I want to stimulate ideas on how you can make small shifts in your mindset to make the most of the opportunities that will come to you in all four areas. So, as you read the rest of the book, ask yourself how each lesson can apply in your personal life, business, community, and career.

When you do, you'll begin to see opportunities everywhere. As you take advantage of those opportunities, you will begin to fulfill your highest and truest self as a human being, and to fulfill the promise of the Creator when he dreamed you into form. There's no telling what the Creator has in store for you. God-sized visions are always bigger than ours. We just need to be open to and aware of the opportunities in the world around us.

- Can you find ways to serve in what you're doing now?
- Will you stay calm and confident through the cycles of life?
- Can you see ways to build your legacy in all four cornerstones of your life?

I know you can because you are a legacy maker.

PART 2

PART 2:
Who Are the Legacy Makers?

Who comes to mind when you think of the phrase *legacy maker?*

If you're like many people, your answer is likely someone wealthy or famous . . . the Oprah Winfreys, Elon Musks, Mother Teresas, or Nelson Mandelas of the world.

You might think of inventors like Thomas Edison, Alexander Graham Bell, or Marie Curie.

You might think of political leaders like Abraham Lincoln, Margaret Thatcher, or Mahatma Gandhi.

And, while none of those answers are *wrong*, they are all incomplete, a fact you learn quickly once you go deeper into what it really means to leave a legacy.

The truth is that legacy makers are more than just wealthy or famous people, inventors, political leaders, and leaders of community or change. They include people whose legacies won't be broadcast on TV or written about in newspapers or online. They include people whose names will never be emblazoned on a billboard or the side of a building. They include people just like you and me, flawed people who work hard, love their family, make mistakes, and worry about the future.

Surprised? I was, too, for a moment, until I dug deeper into what it takes to truly leave a legacy and realized that nowhere in *any* definition of legacy does it include a requirement that a legacy has to be done at scale. Nowhere does it require you to live in a certain city, state, or even country. Nowhere does it require a certain pedigree. Or even a college degree.

There's no IQ test.

There's no blood test.

In every case, the legacies I'm going to tell you about came entirely from what people did—their *actions*.

In this part of the book, I'm going to introduce you to what it takes to become a legacy maker.

I'll show you how anyone—even those of us who are flawed humans—can leave a legacy for their family, friends, community, or even the world. I'll show you how legacy makers are built, not born, and that the level of your commitment to consistently work through the PEACE Legacy Formula will determine your legacy. And I'll show you how you—yes *you*—can become a legacy maker so whenever you leave this world, you will never *truly* leave this world.

By the end, I'm confident you will have a new perspective on how simple it can be for you to leave a legacy on the world that you will be proud of.

I know that you were put on this earth for a reason. We all were.

Your purpose is not just to live your life, turn the calendar a few times, and leave this world no better or different from when you arrived.

You are here for much more than that.

In this part of the book, I'll prove it to you.

Chapter 4:

The Flawed Humans Who Change the World

God chose things the world considers foolish in order to shame those who think they are wise. And he chose things that are powerless to shame those who are powerful.

—APOSTLE PAUL

(1 CORINTHIANS 1:27, NEW LIVING TRANSLATION)

I'd never experienced a blackout while driving before. It was a long drive from Las Vegas to Breckenridge, Colorado, where I planned to stop for the night. The drive had been a pleasure. I always loved long drives in my red 2018 Camaro SS. That car felt like it was part of me.

I first started feeling the weight of drowsiness a few minutes past the city of Vail, but I reasoned that I only had about fifteen more miles to go and kept driving. The last I consciously remember was driving alone on the two-lane freeway before I was awakened out of a blackness to the sound of gravel under my tires; I was off to the side of the freeway. I immediately responded to take control and break. Unfortunately, I was directly in front of one of those thin metal poles used to measure snow depth, and that's all it took. I hit the pole at sixty miles per hour and it destroyed the front bumper, broke off and struck the hood, then bounced over the car breaking the back window on its way. The sensors in the car set off all of the airbags.

I managed to come to a stop on the side of the road, but the car was a total loss. As I sat there, waiting for the inevitable arrival of the police, I was saddened at the loss of the car I loved, but grateful that I was completely unharmed and caused no problems to any other drivers. The police were appropriately, yet unpleasantly, stern with me about my driving and wrote up the strongest ticket they could. They left, and I sat quietly in my car waiting for the tow truck to show up that they'd called for me.

About twenty minutes later, a flatbed tow truck arrived and a bearded man in his early fifties climbed out to greet me. He really felt my pain about the loss of my car but was glad I was OK. He introduced himself as Jack and asked, "Where are you headed? You got a hotel waiting for you?" I told him I was heading for Breckenridge and told him the name of the hotel where I had reservations. After getting the car securely on his flatbed, he offered, "You know, I'm not supposed to do this, but why don't you climb in the cab with me, and I'll drop you off in Breckenridge where you can call an Uber. No taxis are going to come out here to get you."

His caring demeanor was curious and captivating to me. I had to know his story. As we drove, he told me that he'd spent most of his life abusing himself with drugs and alcohol and causing pain to those around him. After a brief stint in jail, he was offered a job as part of his probation to drive a tow truck. He truly felt he was being given a second chance at life and vowed he would do no harm to himself or anyone else ever again. What's more, he wanted to give back to the world in any way he could to make up for the years he'd wasted.

Even more curious, I asked him whether he enjoyed the work he was doing. His response would change my life. He spoke with joy, and a bit tearfully, as he said, "I am living the life of my dreams. Every day I get to be the one who helps people in their real moments of need. And on my days off, I get to ski in the best places on earth. Sometimes I don't feel I deserve this life, but I vow to be of service to everyone I meet."

> *How could a tow truck driver declare that he's living the life of his dreams?*

I was stunned by his answer. In a million years, I never would have thought I'd hear a tow truck driver say he was living the life of his dreams. Meeting Jack was a gift, and I'll never forget him.

I thought to myself how ungrateful I'd been for the life I've been given. If a tow truck driver could find such joy in service, how much more should I appreciate what I have. And, like Jack, shouldn't we all be looking to add even more value to people?

The connection Jack made between driving a tow truck and helping people in real moments of need convinced me that any job, no matter how trivial it may seem, can be fulfilling when done from a heart for service. And if you are already doing great work, I'm equally convinced that you can find even more fulfillment by performing your job with the intention of bettering the lives of those you touch.

Perhaps even more importantly, however, I became convinced that there's no set of minimum qualifications someone needs to achieve before creating a lasting legacy. On that one drive, Jack shared with me a perspective on life that changed the way I thought and acted for the rest of my life. And my changed thoughts and actions created additional ripples, helping countless people live with purpose, find fulfillment, and be remembered.

Jack wasn't a perfect human. Far from it, as he readily admitted. Indeed, he was deeply flawed, having "wasted" the majority of his life, as he put it. But he was a legacy maker in the truest sense of the phrase and I, for one, became a beneficiary of his legacy's life-changing mission.

Whenever I think about Jack, I can't help but be grateful. I'm grateful for having met him. I'm grateful for having started a conversation with him. I'm grateful for his offer to drive me to Breckenridge. I'm grateful most for his willingness to share his story with me, flaws and all.

I'm eternally grateful for having survived that day and for every day I get to share with you on earth. I know a lot of people in similar circumstances weren't that fortunate. In truth, we all should be grateful for every day, as though we were given a second chance at life, even if we didn't drive off the road like I did.

Too Flawed to Change the World?

You show me a person who lived within the last one thousand years who made a world-changing impact and I'll show you a flawed human. From world leaders to inventors, parents to educators, spiritual leaders to community activists, each and every one of them is flawed.

Many of the glamorous stories we read about movie stars or pro athletes don't highlight the struggles, mistakes, and setbacks they endured along the way. Stories talk about their accomplishments, creativity, and hard work. But they often leave out the broken relationships, massive failures, and personal shortcomings and make us feel that they are in a special category that we could never ascend to.

On the other hand, there's no more powerful magnifying glass for imperfections than a simple mirror. When we look in the mirror in the morning, we tend to see all of our wrinkles, scars, and imperfections. Similarly, when we look inside ourselves, we often see our emotional or intellectual wrinkles, scars, and imperfections, yet somehow when we look at other people, we can be blind to see theirs.

If you find yourself struggling with that way of thinking, rest assured that you're not alone. We are all flawed humans who often put our egos and self-interests first. Our primal instinct is for self-preservation, so it's built into us to put ourselves above others. We can't help but compare ourselves to others, looking for how we are superior so we can feel good about where we are in life. Why do you think soap operas have remained so popular? These are instincts we need to overcome and put in their proper place. In the same way, we can't let our natural desires for leisure and comfort guide our actions or we'll end up out of shape and sitting on a couch watching TV all day. Of course, I know you're not the type of person to end up sitting on a couch all day or you wouldn't be reading this book. Just understand that in the same way you discipline your body in spite of its lazy desires, you must also rise above selfish interests and egoic comparisons as your driving motivation.

To shift our focus to service is not natural at first. We don't know who we are without comparison to others, and we want to feel superior in any way we can. That's part of our human identity, albeit a fragile one. As one who grew up in a Christian church, I even observed egoic posturing in who could be more "spiritual" than others. It sounds pathetic to say it, but it's true. Learning to give without a desire for anything in return, or recognition, may feel pointless until we get in touch with our true eternal self. But when service is done from self-interest, it's shallow, and people can feel it.

Moreover, there's a fine line between understanding that everyone is flawed and actively searching for other people's defects. Sometimes, when people begin to truly appreciate that every successful human in history is also truly human, they can begin to train themselves to look for the flaws in others so they can feel superior. Learning that someone respected has chinks in their armor can make some feel better about themselves. Stay out of this trap of comparison. Just know that the flaws are there and, if they succeeded, there's no reason you can't do the same, flaws and all.

The secret is to be self-aware and understand that this is our primal nature: our imperfect self. We have a higher calling, one to live from the supernatural—our spiritual self. In this place, we do what is right, trust the results to our Creator, and remove our attachment to any particular outcome. We're good just knowing we did what we felt was right.

From this place, you will see an impact on others that's genuine. But, in time, you'll see how amazing it is to receive messages from people who thank you for changing their lives and giving them hope. If an ex-convict tow truck driver can find the life of his dreams in service, you can too.

Although I don't actively look for people's flaws and don't recommend you do so either, I've always been fascinated by the dichotomy in the biographies of great people throughout history. Here are just a few examples that showcase what I mean when I say flawed humans can change the world.

STEVE JOBS: One example of a famous and successful man who was also very flawed personally is Steve Jobs, the cofounder and former CEO of Apple Inc. Jobs is widely regarded as a visionary who revolutionized the computer and technology industries with his innovative products such as the Macintosh computer, the iPod, the iPad, and the iPhone.

However, Jobs was also known for his difficult personality and demanding management style, which often resulted in conflicts with colleagues and employees. He could be ruthless in his pursuit of success, and he was known to be critical, impatient, and even abusive toward his employees. Jobs also had a complicated personal life, including a history of denying paternity of his daughter and having a strained relationship with his first wife.

Despite these flaws, Jobs's legacy as a successful entrepreneur and innovator continues to inspire many people in the tech industry and beyond.

WINSTON CHURCHILL: Winston Churchill, the former prime minister of the United Kingdom, is widely regarded as one of the greatest wartime leaders of the twentieth century.

Churchill's leadership during World War II is celebrated for his inspirational speeches, strategic thinking, and refusal to negotiate with the Nazis. However, Churchill was also known for his controversial views and actions, including his opposition to Indian independence and his use of brutal tactics in colonial wars. He also struggled with alcoholism throughout his life and was prone to bouts of depression and mood swings.

Despite these flaws, Churchill's legacy as a wartime leader and his contributions to the defeat of Nazi Germany continue to be celebrated by many people in the United Kingdom and around the world.

ERNEST HEMINGWAY: Another example of a successful but flawed human is Ernest Hemingway, the celebrated American novelist and journalist.

Hemingway is widely regarded as one of the most influential writers of the twentieth century, known for his spare, straightforward writing style and his portrayal of the "lost generation" of expatriates in Europe after World War I. However, he also had a tumultuous personal life, marked by heavy drinking, numerous romantic relationships, and a tendency toward depression and suicidal thoughts.

Hemingway's troubled personal life was reflected in some of his writing, including his novel *The Sun Also Rises*, which explores themes of disillusionment and alcoholism. Despite his flaws, Hemingway's literary contributions have had a lasting impact on American literature, and he remains a celebrated figure in the world.

And the list goes on! You get the idea. You don't have to be perfect to serve, have an impact on the world, and find your life to be truly satisfying. But there's even more. I believe that you've already been given something great to do in this world and all of the resources needed to make it happen. And I see it as your responsibility to discover and release it to the world—to do the good work that you are called to do.

Look in Your Heart

I've often said, "If it's in your heart, it's already yours." I say that because I believe that the things you have been called to do radiate from deep within you. They are given to you by your Creator. Another way to think about it is to imagine asking God this question: "What did you imagine for me when you created me?" Would you be ready for his answer? Would you be scared of what he would tell you? Would you act upon it no matter what he said?

To truly receive your answer, you will need to do four things:

1. Surrender your ego to a higher calling
2. Learn how to listen to the still, small voice within
3. Have faith that a dream has been given to you

4. Believe that everything you need for making it a reality has also been provided

Surrender my ego? What even *is* an ego? I know there are many ideas and definitions, but I want to offer one for our purposes. Your ego is simply your human identity. When you introduce yourself to people, you may offer your name, what you do for a living, something about your family, where you live, or some of your accomplishments. These are all part of our human experience, true, but they are not our true identities. For example, if you decided to go by another name, would you still be you? Of course you would. If you changed careers, would you still be you? You would. When your children are grown and gone, who are you then? You're still you. And your accomplishments of the past may be beautiful parts of your legacy, but is that all there is to you? Of course not.

Your true identity is that of an eternal spirit living out life in a human existence, with a Creator who has amazing plans for you, just like he has amazing plans for me. Our purpose here is to offer hope, encouragement, delight, and love to our fellow human beings. We have all of the resources already available within us to accomplish great things. We often just need to know how to look for them and even *what* to look for. Our task is to learn how to listen, be guided, and act boldly knowing that unseen forces will come to our aid, often through a still, small voice of wisdom.

How do we learn to listen for (and to) that still, small voice of wisdom? First, you have to understand that it is always there hoping to communicate with you. We've all had times when we said, "My gut told me not to do it, and I did it anyway. I should have listened to my gut." This is an example of what I'm talking about. You can develop the skills to listen and, hopefully, respond to the prompting to do the right thing.

Listening requires quiet and intention. I think you'll find that forms of meditation are practiced by all great achievers. Why? After a time of quieting your mind, you can enter a state of tranquility. It's a calm confidence that allows you to ask the right questions and get instinctive answers.

Look into the Future

Matthew McConaugheyonce said that, before he makes a decision, he imagines his life as if he said yes to the opportunity offered to him to see how he felt about it and how his decision would impact his life. He lives with this visualization as if it were real, lives with it for a day with full emotions, and sees how he feels about that course of action. Next, he'll imagine saying no to the opportunity and look at how that decision would impact his life and how he feels about that. In fully living out both options, he gets a sense of peace and knowing which is the better course of action to take. I couldn't think of a better example of how to listen to your inner voice of wisdom. We'll go deeper into all of this in chapter 14.

Finally, when you feel in your heart that you know what direction you should take, expect that help will come, but also be prepared for resistance.

Taking action, any action, in the direction of your dream is the essence of being fully alive. Your "inner warriors" will jump to life. You'll not want to do anything else. It will fire you up and open your mind to see even more opportunities. Faith comes from believing that in acting boldly, unseen forces will come to your aid. The world stands aside for the person with passion. Unique "coincidences" will pop up in your daily life. It's exhilarating! The key, however, is that you go all-in. Legacy isn't something you can dabble in. You don't stumble into living with purpose, finding fulfillment, and building a legacy through which you will be remembered.

In everything you do, do it with everything you have!

Anticipate Resistance

As you move forward to build an incredible legacy, be aware that you *will* experience resistance. It may come from people close to you, or trolls and critics, or from technical obstacles, but it *will* come. And when you naturally harbor some level of doubt, as just about all flawed humans do, it is natural to be tempted to question whether you should continue.

You need to be ready for the resistance and the emotional responses it creates. Don't be surprised by them. Expect them. And train yourself to react to those not by giving up but by doubling down. Treat these as times to re-up your determination to get the job done. It just won't always be pleasant or easy. Of course you'd love to have everyone you know on board and cheering you on. It can be disappointing to feel you have to go on your journey alone. Some legacy makers do have great support at home. Others go at it alone for a while and build community with other like-minded legacy makers through mastermind groups or other communities.

Resistance can come from all directions. You might have support at home but experience technical or other situational difficulties. You might experience a key partner letting you down. I've seen all of these and more. I've had betrayals, had people steal from me, and many other obstacles. In one case, it took me three years before I could see everything working out after a major setback. In those moments, I am grateful to myself that I didn't give up. It was all worth it.

The greatest words of encouragement I can offer are just to love yourself exactly how you are, flaws and all. Accept your missteps and know that they aren't fatal. Failures along the way are course corrections guiding you to the better path for seeing your dreams come true. Appreciate that your past failures helped make you into who you are today, and what you do today, tomorrow, and the next day will determine who you become in the future.

You are flawed. So what? Everyone is. The difference between the legacy maker and others is that you know the good your dreams will do and you don't quit. You get started. You are values-driven. And you can—and *will*—keep going.

Other than that, we are all the same. Love your flawed fellow humans, too, even if they are not actively pursuing the same legacy making that you are. They're on their own path and they have to live with themselves. You want to live with and love yourself knowing that you are already making a difference and that difference will only grow as you continue down your path to building your legacy and changing the world.

Chapter 5:

Legacy Makers Are Built, Not Born

Leaders are made, they are not born. They are made by hard effort, which is the price which all of us must pay to achieve any goal that is worthwhile.
—VINCE LOMBARDI

You were born into this world with a blank slate. What you do with your life is completely up to you, even if it may not feel that way at times. Yes, some people are born into privilege while others are born into terrible conditions. Oprah Winfrey was born into poverty and racial hatred. She was sexually abused for years in her childhood, yet she rose above it, determined to bring light to as many people as she could through sharing real-life stories.

Some people are born into wealth and spend it on self-indulgence, while others take it as a challenge to do even greater things for the world than their parents did.

It's easy to use your lineage as an excuse for where you are or how high you have to climb. Can you imagine if your father was doing time for murder? How would you escape the shadow of your father's past to build your own name? On the other hand, what if your father or mother were loved and famous around the world? How would you develop a name for yourself then?

Listen, the beauty is that you have just as much of an ability to build a legacy as anyone else. You might have less money while others have an abundance. Some people might have less time while others might have more time. Some have good health while others suffer from chronic conditions. You have your advantages and disadvantages, and they have theirs.

The truth is clear: no one is born with a legacy. You might be born to someone who made a legacy for themselves, but you get to choose whether to build upon it or deviate from it and go a different path. No one comes into this world with a legacy already established. Truly, legacy makers are built, not born.

In the 2006 movie *Rocky Balboa*, there is a classic scene where Rocky's son is complaining that his father's fame was a big cloud over his head that didn't give him any space to discover his own path. Rocky responds to him with these famous words:

> When the time came for you to be your own man and take on the world, and you did. But somewhere along the line you changed. You stopped being you. You let people stick a finger in your face and tell you you're no good. And when things got hard, you started looking for something to blame; like a big shadow.

> Let me tell you something you already know. The world ain't all sunshine and rainbows. It's a very mean and nasty place. And I don't care how tough you are, it will beat you to your knees and keep you there permanently if you let it. You, me, or nobody is going to hit as hard as life. But it ain't about how hard you hit; it's about how hard you can get hit and keep moving forward. How

much you can take and keep moving forward. That's how winning is done!

Now, if you know what you're worth, then go out and get what you're worth. But you've gotta be willing to take the hits and not pointing fingers saying you ain't where you want to be because of him or her or anybody. Cowards do that and that ain't you! You're better than that!

I'm always going to love you no matter what happens. You're my son and you're my blood. You're the best thing in my life. But, until you start believing in yourself, you ain't going to have a life.

DNA has no impact on your legacy. It's not what you inherit that matters. It's what you create from the internal gifts you were given that are yours alone. You don't inherit your calling from your parents. You're given one of your own to reveal to the world.

Know this: creating a legacy must be done with intention. People can go through life just showing up at their jobs, doing life, and going on occasional vacations and never be remembered for having been here after they're gone. Others can also do small things every day that add up to something great that will impact the world around them. It just takes intentionality. It's nurture, not nature, to create your unique mark on the world.

Legacy Makers Are Passionate about Their Pursuit

Silicon Valley in the late '90s was a time in history like none other. The energy was like being on a Red Bull 24/7. I was thirty-five and had my shot at writing a business plan for an idea I had, but I was clearly in over my head. I mentioned this story in chapter 2, but I wanted to add one more insight here.

My dad wanted to give me some help in floating my business idea around, so he introduced me to one of the members at his church by the name of Mario Rosati. Mario just happened to also be a founding partner at Wilson Sonsini Goodrich & Rosati, a major Silicon Valley law firm with more than nine hundred attorneys on staff. They were at the center of many of the biggest venture capital deals and were known around the world.

In one of my early meetings with Mario, I asked him what he looked for when listening to a pitch. His answer was life-changing to me: "The first thing we look at is the person presenting. We're looking for that person who is so filled with conviction in their idea that we realize they are going to make it happen with or without us. It then becomes our choice to participate or not. That's what we want. It's first about their passion and conviction. The fundamentals are important, of course, but it won't see the light of day in the hands of someone without that inner drive."

Nothing replaces passion. Hard work alone is not enough. You need to believe that your efforts matter and must come to life or you'll die trying.

I'd often heard it said that there were only two motivations in life: the pursuit of pleasure and the avoidance of pain. I believe there is a third: pure passion. When you are passionate about something, you don't care about pleasure or pain. You are driven to see your vision come to life no matter the setbacks or incremental victories along the way. Pain and pleasure are less important than *the drive to see your vision come to life*.

Steve Jobs once said, "Apple is not about making boxes for people to get their jobs done, although we do that well. Apple is about something more. Its core value is that we believe that people with passion can change the world for the better."

Yes, people with passion can change the world. In fact, I believe that the world takes notice of people with passion. People want to join their causes. It's a way of living that, once you've experienced it, you wouldn't want to live any other way.

If you don't have a great passion project you're working on, then start by doing whatever you're doing now with excellence and let that become your reputation. King Solomon was said to be the wisest man who ever lived. He said it in this way three thousand years ago, "Whatever your hand finds to do, do it with all of your might" (Eccles. 9:10, New International Version). Excellence will often attract the opportunities to you that may end up becoming your big opportunity. People reward those who dare greatly and execute.

Legacy Makers Take Action

When I turned twenty-five, my father gave me a birthday card with the quote I mentioned earlier: "Act boldly and unseen forces will come to your aid." I kept that card on my desk in front of me for years and found it to be a profound influence on my life. I've often joked with friends of mine that luck is my superpower. In reality, I find that fortuitous "coincidences" come to people who act boldly and believe in divine assistance. They may come in the form of people you meet or with "lucky breaks," but nothing comes from nothing. Action is required; any action.

I've often said that all we are required to do is what we can, when we can, for as long as we can. But how many people do?

Action is also your proving ground. That's where you make the mistakes to learn what will actually work and what won't. I personally think that most initial ideas for projects will end up bearing little resemblance to what ends up working in the end, but you'll never arrive at that final success if you don't start.

I grew up hearing it said that "Anything worth doing is worth doing well," but that's not reality. I love how Les Brown said it, which was essentially that *anything worth doing is worth doing terribly until you can do it well*. When you first started learning to drive a car, it was a nerve-racking experience. You panicked trying to remember everything and not hit other cars along the way. Today, you can drive without even paying attention to it. But we forget how we started. Yet, it's how we start and learn anything, so expect your first actions to feel unfamiliar and uncomfortable and that you won't be good at them.

You've probably been told that you have to leave your comfort zone to do anything of significance. But what that will mean in real life is that you're always moving into new territory. That nervous energy from charting courses into the unknown should be a regular part of your life if you are truly growing and expanding as a person. But don't let the nervous energy stop you. Personally, I feel that if I'm not pushing myself into new territory, it means that I'm getting too comfortable.

Action is a gift that gives you guidance and excitement in life. Learning to love the daily process of progress is the key to all success. The day of final accomplishment is simply a moment in time. Yes, it's a time for celebration, but you can't wait for new excitement that will come from taking action again the next day. *You can't wait for everything to be perfect to be happy.* "Enjoy the journey" is truly a motto for success.

List your next action steps, take one, and celebrate that it brings you one step closer to your goals and then take the next.

Common Regrets of People in Their Nineties

I was fortunate enough to hear a lecture on this topic when I was in my twenties. There were three main regrets mentioned by the speaker, and I want to share those with you now. No matter what your age, you can learn from the wisdom of those who have gone before you and are close to finishing their race.

While researching for this book, I found many studies that have been done in listing the regrets shared by those in their nineties, but the list I was given so many years ago seems to have captured the essence of all of them. Here they are:

1. I wish I'd risked more.
2. I wish I'd enjoyed each season of life more.
3. I wish I'd done more to leave a legacy.

I Wish I'd Risked More

How many of us have had a business or product idea, but we didn't follow up on it, only to see someone else make it later and make it big? "I had that idea!" we say. In most cases, what held people back was fear. Good ideas will find money. Good ideas will find people to help make them come true. Some people even get started, but they give up too soon.

I had one of those stories. Ken was a friend from church who had been a popular DJ in the '80s and '90s and knew many key people in the music business. I had seen how Myspace was floundering and lost its identity, which gave me an idea. What if people could create their own music stations based on the music they loved and share their stations with their friends? It would be funded by advertising that they selected. Perhaps they loved Pepsi, Nike, and Levi's. We'd create imaginative and humorous ads and feed music to their channels based on their personal likes. Ken had access to the world library of music. We were going to call our program Symfonix.

However, when push came to shove, Ken wanted the concept to be patented before we could move forward. In all, it would have taken about $20K in legal fees to get it done, so we dropped the idea. Over the next few years, we'd see start-up after start-up create music apps and sites that allowed people to create their own music mixes. If I'd persisted, we would have been the first to market. I allowed outside influences to tell me whether something would or wouldn't work, without even trying. Most people have similar stories of ideas they had that they didn't act upon only to later watch as someone else produced it and made millions. Do you have a story like that? What have you wanted to do that you know you should have done but didn't?

Vow to yourself not to have one of these regrets, as so many in their nineties did, that they should have risked more. Let that fear of regret fuel you to at least try.

I Wish I'd Enjoyed Each Season of Life More

It doesn't take much explanation to understand this regret. We've all been there. I remember my frustration in my twenties: always feeling like I wasn't as far in life as I wanted to be. I was always looking for that next raise or opportunity, focusing on buying a house or getting the kids into school, etc. I was the classic example of "I'll be happy when . . ." The problem is that life passes us by while we're waiting for the next season to come. Kids get older. We don't value what we have along the way.

There was a classic episode of the original *Dick Van Dyke Show* where he is having dinner with his wife, Laura, and emotionally venting about his frustrations from the day at the office. At the end of dinner, after dessert, he stopped abruptly and declared, "Wait! What was that? Was that pecan pie? It's my favorite and I missed it!" Yes, he ate it but was completely unaware because he was letting the temporary frustrations of his day dominate his focus.

Every season of life is precious. I know of so many successful entrepreneurs who talk fondly about the days of struggle and setback that ended up being the most meaningful to them. But, at the time, they just wanted to get to the next phase of their quest. Wouldn't it be amazing if we could learn to value every season *while we're in it*? Can we learn to love the struggle in its season, and not just years later in reflection?

Whether you want to call it, "taking time to smell the roses," or by any other name, the wisdom of our soul tells us the same. Be fully present in the season we're in and with the people around us.

I Wish I'd Done More to Leave a Legacy

I'm so glad to have you on this journey with me. Just the fact that you bought this book, you've obviously already felt the calling to do more to be a legacy maker, so you'll never have this regret.

To me, this has got to be one of the saddest commentaries of a life lived for so many decades on earth: to wonder whether my time here even mattered.

As we've learned, creating a legacy does not happen by accident. It's made with intention. You've got this.

In the next chapter, we'll dive into what it takes to become the legacy maker you were destined to be. We're on a roll!

Chapter 6:

You: The Making of a Legacy Maker

Character cannot be developed in ease and quiet.
Only through experience of trial and suffering can the soul be
strengthened, ambition inspired, and success achieved.
—HELEN KELLER

A t 5:30 a.m. on February 24, 2022, I was awakened out of my sleep in Mykolaiv, Ukraine, to the thunderous sound of explosions. The ground shook. It was really happening. The Russians had begun their attack and invasion. It was all very real.

I'd been living in Ukraine for most of the previous eight years, enjoying family, business, and our philanthropic work with the orphanages there. Ukraine is a beautiful country filled with hard-working people who love family above all. We'd been regularly hearing the threats of war since 2014 but supposed, as before, that it was all just political posturing again. We woke up that day and understood clearly that war was upon us.

My mind raced to think what the day might bring. I quickly drove to my office and sent out a short video message to let people know that the war had started, then jumped into practical action. On the first day, people lined up at ATMs to get what cash they could. The lines at grocery stores and gas stations were hours long. No one knew how long supplies would last.

I made a trip to the closest orphanage we supported to see what they needed. They only had five days' worth of food and medicine left to care for more than one hundred children under four years of age. They had been expecting deliveries the following day from Kherson, but we all realized it wouldn't be coming. So I gathered a few of my team members and raced to the grocery stores and pharmacies to get what we could.

During those first few weeks, we witnessed incredible acts of kindness as people who had been in line for an hour at the grocery store allowed us to enter before them knowing we were shopping for the kids. Gas stations were closed, so we called the corporate owners to ask whether they could give us fuel from their reserves—and they did. On one trip to the hospital to get medical supplies, we ran into a group of Ukrainian soldiers. When they learned we were with the orphanage, they gave us two hundred pounds of potatoes from their own food rations to feed the children.

These were defining moments for me. As a human being, you would hope you'd act in a manner of which you would be proud when such things happen, but you never truly know until it happens. I had many friends and family members who were urging me to get out of the country for months leading up to the war. But I told them I had to stay. As a US citizen, it would have been pretty easy for me to flee before the war started or even immediately after the war started. But I clearly recognized the work that was needed to stabilize the orphanages' operations, knowing that war could become the new norm.

Even though I wasn't convinced that the Russians would invade, I made the choice to stay months before it happened. I had three primary reasons for deciding to stay:

1. I couldn't bear the thought of being safe in the US and just watching on a big screen TV at home as my employees, friends, and extended family were dealing with the horrors of war.
2. I wanted to be able to look back one year later and be proud of myself for what I did.
3. I believed that if I was there, I was there for a reason. I was meant to be there for such a time as this, to do what good I could while I could.

I spent the next seven months after the invasion driving to many cities across Ukraine to assess the needs of more than twenty orphanages, arranging for deliveries of food and medicine, and helping them all adjust to the "new normal."

Most of these orphanages were forced to set up living arrangements in the basements and bomb shelters since air raid sirens were going off four or five times every day. Every night we could hear the sounds of artillery and bombs exploding in the distance. At night, the cities would go into complete blackout and curfews were strictly enforced.

Before the War

After the Invasion

One night I didn't make it back to my apartment before the 10:00 p.m. curfew and was pulled over by a squad of soldiers with military assault rifles. As they angrily yelled at me in Ukrainian, all I could do was lie on the ground with my arms out by my sides and try to explain myself in English. I was a bit freaked out. I tried to explain that I was just one block from my apartment, but they didn't understand a word I was saying. They called in a soldier who spoke English to translate, and they allowed me to get to my apartment under escort. The danger was very real, but it never caused me a moment of hesitation. The orphanages' needs were greater than my own.

In the end, we continued to bring aid to the orphanages in Ukraine, including five that came under Russian control in the Kherson region. It took amazing work by many heroic individuals to navigate such difficult but important goals. I'm very proud of the work we did and continue to do there.

I hadn't considered how this would affect me at the time. I was just doing whatever was required each day. Eventually, we set up support systems near each facility so we could continue support from the US. Low fuel supplies were making it riskier to drive long distances.

As I collected my thoughts, I realized how this work is part of my legacy. In fact, I think that the study I'd previously done on being a legacy maker changed my focus and perspective on everything. Without it, I'm not sure whether I would have left much earlier.

The book in your hands is more than your typical self-help book. It will develop in you a new character as a person. You will instinctively act based on service. You will become the hero in your own story.

Becoming a legacy maker carries with it a nobility of character. You see the impact on others and the long-term implications of your decisions. It will be second nature to you, and you'll be proud of who you become.

As I thought about the character traits of legacy makers, three came to mind:

- Legacy makers are others-focused.
- Legacy makers are long-term thinkers.
- Legacy makers have strong morning rituals.

Legacy Makers Are Others-Focused

It's not in our nature to think in terms of service. The core drive deep in our survival instincts is for self-preservation, not for the needs of others. It takes maturity and spiritual awareness to see the needs around you. But this is what legacy makers do because they realize that their legacies are about what others will say about how they added value to their lives.

You can't serve with the goal of getting pats on the back from others. Service that comes from a motivation to feed our egos is short-lived. People have highly tuned BS detectors. Authenticity, on the other hand, resonates in people's hearts. We are all very human and focus on our own needs first, but the legacy maker develops a genuine desire to make a difference in other people's lives.

The secret to cultivating a focus on others is awareness. However, it's more than just an awareness of the needs of the people we encounter; it's also an awareness of the greater challenges that may be hitting our world at large.

David is in one of my coaching groups and he shared this story. He was making a long drive from California to the high desert of New Mexico. Fifteen hours into his drive, the red "engine" light came on in his car, and he felt the car begin to slowly lose power and stop. He turned off the car and started to become really angry. "Why me? Now I'm stranded in the middle of the desert at 1:00 a.m. with no cell coverage!" There were no other cars on the road to lend assistance either. He was truly alone.

He got out of the car and started to walk. He had no choice, really. Ahead in the distance he could see a light, like a streetlamp, but just one and nothing else. After two miles of walking toward the light, he could see what it was. It was an entrance to a military base with a guard post beneath the streetlamp. As he approached, a wary soldier called to him to declare his business. He explained the situation and the guard agreed to let him use his phone to make a call. But who would he call at this time of night? He had a friend who lived about forty minutes from there, so that was his one hope.

However, when he called, his friend's wife answered the phone. After hearing his plight, she offered to help. She got directions to his location and was there an hour later to give him a ride. Once in the car, he began to express his frustrations, but she stopped him firmly and declared that he had been an answer to her prayer! Perplexed, he asked, "What? I got you up in the middle of the night to come get me. How am I the answer to your prayer?"

"David, my husband and I had a huge fight last night and I was lying in bed praying to God to give me an excuse to get out of the house for a while so I could cool down. I didn't want to say anything I'd later regret. I just needed some time and space, and at that very moment, you called."

He recalled the story to me and asked, "Is it really possible that God knew she would be praying for help right as I arrived at the guard post? Had he really arranged my situation so I would be calling her at that very moment?" In deep reflection, he said, "Maybe my frustration was someone else's answer to prayer. Perhaps this entire situation was not about me at all. I was an angel of love for her."

What if we were able to look at the events of our day in that light, that the people and events that come our way each day may be opportunities arranged for us to offer an expression of kindness? This mindset changes your heart and focus and can add a new meaning to all of your encounters each day. Think about it. Becoming service-minded becomes second nature when you decide that it's important for you to be aware of what's going on around you. It's that simple.

Legacy Makers Are Long-Term Thinkers

It's understood that your legacy is a compilation of your life's work and how you touched people in a positive way. By definition, legacy makers are long-term thinkers. Your legacy is the culmination of your life experiences.

"A society grows great when old men plant trees whose shade they know they shall never sit in." That version of the quote comes from an ancient Greek proverb that captures a timeless truth about the value of long-term thinking and selfless action for the greater good.

A different take on the theme is this: "The seeds you plant today will grow into trees that bear fruit for others to be nourished by." The question is, "What kinds of seeds are you planting?" There will be some kind of fruit produced from our actions, but not all fruit is edible or nourishing.

As a legacy maker, I think you intuitively know these things to be true. I don't feel that I need to add more to it, but I didn't want to leave it unsaid either.

Now, let's talk about something very practical: what you do every day that makes you even more into the legacy maker you want to become.

Legacy Makers Have Strong Morning Rituals

This is where it all becomes real—where the rubber meets the road. Legacy creation must be built into our daily rituals. How you start your day sets the tone, as you're probably well aware. But I'll suggest a morning routine to help you integrate your legacy making into your daily life, and we'll get them done in thirty minutes or less.

Here are the key elements of the morning ritual:

- Meditation
- Gratitude practice
- Legacy Action Items
- Micro-visualizations
- Reading and journaling

Meditation

I was never into the idea of meditation. It seemed really "woo-woo" to me, for tree huggers and crystal worshippers. I finally got some good information on why I would want to meditate and the tangible benefits. I'd like to share what I have learned and the easiest form of meditation imaginable that really works.

The purpose of meditation is to gain self-control, quiet your mind, and calm your nervous system. I realized I'd spent most of my life waking up every morning with nervous energy and my mind spinning on tasks for the day and problems from yesterday. I'd immediately reach for my phone to see whether anyone needed me or whether I'd missed anything I should have done. In other words, I started every day stressed and anxious about everything. My mind would be running scenarios within minutes of being awake. Every day felt like I was putting out one fire after another.

Meditation changed all of that once I understood the objective. Think of it this way. You know intuitively that you have to tell your body that it's not in control, and not give in to every desire. Many people start with cold dips or showers. As much as the body hates it, you are telling it that you are in control. When you make it to the gym, even though your body is screaming to sleep more, you affirm control again. After a while, your whining body stops fighting you as much and the discipline becomes easier.

There is an interesting battle that goes on with your thoughts when you meditate. This is where you must win the battle over your mind. You'll have thoughts come that tell you to stop and attend to something urgent. But you'll keep focused on your breathing and continue. Then it will tell you that you don't have time for this, but you continue unfazed. Finally, it might try to sympathize with you and say, "Let's stop and journal some beautiful thoughts." But you don't stop until your mind realizes it's not going to win and that you're in charge. At that moment, a powerful feeling will come to you; it's a sense of calm control and a heart filled with love and gratitude.

Personally, I set a timer for twenty minutes to do my meditation. Some days it may take more, others less, but I continue until I arrive at that place of calm control. It's a force that will carry you through your entire day.

The meditation practice I use is simple. Find a quiet place and sit comfortably. You may have your feet on the floor or crossed. Whatever is comfortable for you so you're not thinking about it. You can sit with your back slightly arched, just don't lean back into the chair if possible. Your hands can be palms up and resting on each other at some place in your lap. Some people put on a headset and listen to the sounds of nature.

I use a breathing technique known as "box breathing." Breath in through your nose and out through your mouth. You'll inhale and hold with a full diaphragm, meaning belly out. Just hold as long as feels comfortable, maybe just a few seconds. Then exhale through your mouth, empty your lungs, and hold. Then repeat the cycle. It helps to do something with your mind while breathing. You can count; "1" while inhaling, "2" and hold, "3" exhale, and "4" at the hold with emptied lungs. Each cycle may take fifteen seconds or so.

Continue until you feel the nervous tension in your body give way to calm and peace. Your mind will be quiet and your heart will open.

Now you're in the right place to go to the next step.

Gratitude Practice

Another practice I was late to integrate into my life was a gratitude practice. Since I grew up as a pastor's kid, I equated gratitude with the prayer we'd say before a meal. It seemed like an empty ritual. Would I just thank God for the day, the food, and the fact that I was alive? That's a great form of respect, but very different from a gratitude practice.

As I grew as a personal development coach, one thing became clear to me: what we focus on becomes our reality. As you've heard it said, "Where focus goes, energy flows." It dawned on me that I'm always attracting into my life more of what I focus on with emotion. Most mornings I would wake up emotionally connected to stress, overwhelm, and fear of failing someone. So, you can guess what my days were like.

Then it occurred to me: "What if I focused on things I loved in my life? Wouldn't I attract more of those things?" Of course I would! This was a real breakthrough for me.

I began my gratitudes by including things about myself that I liked or wanted to grow into. I'm thankful that I am so deeply loved by God. I am thankful for a sound mind. I'm thankful for being resilient and finishing what I start. I am grateful for the spirit of love I have for my fellow humans. Then I'll get really specific. I'll express gratitude for certain people in my life or a new adventure I'm looking forward to.

Pick three that feel strongest and write those down.

Legacy Action Items

Taking small, daily steps in each of the five areas of the Legacy PEACE formula will create a lifestyle for you as a legacy maker. Incremental progress compounds over a lifetime to create greatness. Even though we'll take a deeper dive into these five areas in Part 3 of the book, consider it your standard operating procedure to include this into your Legacy morning routine.

- People: Who will you touch base with today to maintain contact with those in your immediate circles? Who will you connect with today to forward a project or initiative?

- Experiences: What upcoming events are you planning for? Do you need to take a step forward today?

- Assets: Is today the day you take inventory of your cash and investments? Is there a small step you can take?

- Creations: How are your creative projects going? Do you need to allocate focus time to work on one of them?

- Expressions of Kindness: What can you do today to make someone's day?

It's easy to see how the new priority you are putting on your legacy will make a shift in your mindset. You become what you focus on consistently. You are becoming a legacy maker with your daily habits. You will make time for what is important to you. You may not have something to do in every area each day, but awareness is the key. What could be more important to consider in the planning of your day than your impact on the world. This is where you make your legacy happen.

Micro-Visualizations

Now we have a chance to do something very specific to make our days awesome. I call these micro-visualizations. This is the magical practice of pre-living part of your day and seeing it going so well that you'll be looking forward to it! You've seen athletes do this before events, when they close their eyes and pre-live the event in their mind. The downhill Olympic skiers are the most fun to watch when they're preparing for their run. They close their eyes and you see their head and bodies shift from side to side as they imagine every turn in their minds before doing it in real life. Have you thought about doing the same leading into a sales call you will be making today?

Here's your assignment. Pick three things you know you'll be doing today. For example, you may have a day that includes a business presentation, drinks with friends after work, and a call with your mother later that night. Most people just put those on their calendar and walk into each without a lot of forethought. What if you were to preplay your presentation in your mind? Imagine it being powerful, fun, energetic, and enthusiastically received. Imagine it vividly with full emotions from the moment you walk in the room. See the faces of your colleagues being supportive and engaged. When the time comes to give that presentation, don't you think you'd be more comfortable and confident when presenting? Would your presentation be better? Would your chances of creating that outcome be dramatically increased compared with not doing this exercise?

How would your time with friends be improved if you imagined truly enjoying your time with them so everyone wanted to do it again soon after? Imagine it being that way in advance. How would your call with your mother be improved if you had an intention that she felt warmth from the call, and that you could end the call when needed?

It only takes about one minute for each, but it will make quantum improvements in how those events go and create a positive anticipation that this is going to be a great day. You're now energetically looking forward to several things in your day!

Reading and Journaling

You may have heard it said many times before that we become like the five people we spend the most time with. But have you ever considered that some of those people can be authors, thinkers, and podcasters you invite into your mind through their books and content? This is the easiest way to elevate your thinking and expectations for yourself. You're spending time with real achievers and absorbing their beliefs and strategies.

In addition to the self-help books you may be reading, use this meditation time to add some wisdom literature. You can read excerpts from the Bible, quotes from the ancient stoics, or personal development books or audiobooks. Taking in deeper thoughts of wisdom is a perfect way to bookend your personal time.

Finally, make sure you jot down whatever insights you gleaned from your reading and intentions. You'll have lost them by midday if you don't.

This entire process takes about thirty to forty minutes in your morning to complete, but it will transform your days and your character. You'll operate from a calm confidence and deep wisdom you wouldn't trade for anything.

To make this even easier for you, I've created a daily journal template you can download for free at MarcumDavis.com/Legacy. In it, you'll be able to incorporate aspects of the PEACE Legacy Formula that you plan into your day, plus your gratitude practice and micro-visualizations. Add to that places for charting your schedule, to-do list, and an open page for journaling and reflection, and it's a powerful way to keep you focused on what really matters to you every day. Download it, start to implement it, and shoot me an email to let me know how it most benefits you.

Creating Space for Legacy Making

Let's face it, for most of us, we've already found ways to fill our days. Our plates are already full. But what are they full of? What is on your plate now? In order for you to do more, you have to make room for more, meaning something on the plate may need to go to create space for legacy making activities.

Not doing this should concern you more than making time for it. You don't want to have any regrets later in life, nor do you want to see any day lived that doesn't take at least some small steps forward. And living in a state of nervous energy and putting out fires is not going to give you the kind of day you want.

I'm only talking about thirty minutes or so to start the kind of day you'll be looking forward to. Sleep less if you must, but decide now to make this a nonnegotiable practice.

These thirty-minute rituals are the training grounds for your greatness. It's in solitude that all habits are formed, whether it be practicing guitar, writing, working out, or any other skill. You will be recognized later as outstanding for the private daily practices that are not seen or recognized in public.

Can your greatness be found in a thirty-minute daily practice? Without a doubt, yes. No question.

Build Your Best Body

The Dalai Lama (Tenzin Gyatso), when asked what surprised him most about humanity, answered, "Man! Because he sacrifices his health in order to make money. Then he sacrifices money to recuperate his health. And then he is so anxious about the future that he does not enjoy the present; the result being that he does not live in the present or the future; he lives as if he is never going to die, and then dies having never really lived."

I lived as an obese man for most of my life. At age fifty-three, I was rudely awakened by seeing a photo of the body I had created. I was enormous. I had to wear shirts untucked and draped over me like a muumuu. I had to take naps in the afternoons and struggled with foggy thinking. Even more, I learned that I was prediabetic, and I had high cholesterol and high blood pressure. My doctor told me I was less than five years from a life-threatening incident, such as a stroke or heart attack, if I didn't make some drastic changes. I vowed at that moment that I'd never be that man again! I changed my diet and exercised six days a week.

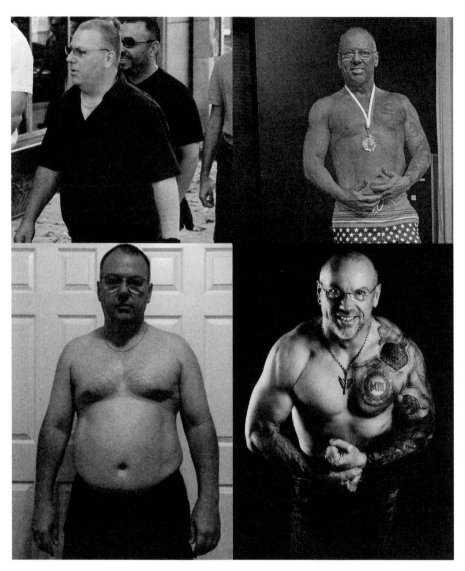

We have many excuses in the West for living in poor health. We don't think we have time to go to the gym or exercise. There is unhealthy food everywhere, and good nutrition means personal time to prepare and cook. But, in truth, I was losing hours of every day in drowsiness, naps, and loss of mental focus. I gained all of that time and energy back once I regained my health. We have the time to do what is important to us—always.

If you need help in this area, I've created a line of supplements, a fitness app, and more at AuthenticStrength.com. The app was designed so you can just show up and do what is shown for that day. There are programs designed for every level of fitness. The programs I share have helped many people improve their health, and some have even lost more than 100 pounds of fat; one man lost 160 pounds! The purpose of Authentic Strength is to create a community of people dedicated to living vibrantly and becoming their best. I'm very proud of you for wanting to live with passion. We'll help.

Add years to your life. Remain active and vibrant. We need you to be with us for years to come. You deserve to enjoy life in a healthy body. It's your responsibility, to yourself and the rest of us, to do the best with what you have been given.

This is one tip I can promise will add value to all other aspects of your life. You're worth it.

PART 3

PART 3:

How to Build Your Legacy— The **PEACE** Legacy Formula

P eace. How does it feel to read that word?

Is it calming? Encouraging?

Imagine your life, full of peace. Peace from the mistakes of your past. Peace in the present. And peace about the future.

Take a moment and think about it. Sit in silence for a moment and imagine you have moved on from past mistakes and experiences.

Imagine being content in the present moment, even as you pursue more and better relationships, experiences, and achievements moving forward.

Imagine understanding that you might not be able to predict *exactly* what your future will look like, but being confident that your future will be better than your past, and knowing that when you leave the world, your memory will live on in others for generations to come.

Peace.

It's not just the feeling you will experience when you build your legacy.

It's the process it takes to build your legacy in the first place.

Peace in the present frees you from the mistakes of the past.

Peace in the present brings you comfort and joy in the present.

And peace in the present gives you hope and excitement for the future.

I've already introduced you to the PEACE Legacy Formula in the introduction and briefly discussed how you can use it to build your legacy.

I've already told you the truth about legacies, what they are, how they help you achieve true, enduring greatness, and the four cornerstones of legacy that legacy makers develop.

I've already shown how legacy makers are no richer, smarter, or more connected than you. They are all flawed human beings just like you and me.

In this part, I'm going to walk you through each element of the PEACE Legacy Formula and show you exactly how to build your legacy, step-by-step, starting right where you are, without needing any additional time or money. This is the deep dive you've been waiting for.

First, we'll talk about the people you need in your life and how to build richly satisfying relationships with them.

Next, we'll talk about creating memorable experiences. After all, we are the sum of our stories.

Then, we'll talk about assets you can start accumulating today—even if you are just getting started building wealth. Assets are the currency of dreams.

After that, we'll talk about creations you can make to share your gifts with the world.

And, finally, we'll talk about how to use simple expressions of kindness to find more peace in the present and keep your legacy alive long into the future. It's a lifestyle of service.

That's all it takes to find peace in the present and build a lasting legacy.

None of it requires millions of dollars or thousands of hours.

None of it's complicated.

And you can start doing all of them today.

By finding peace, through PEACE.

Chapter 7:

People: The Riches in Relationships

*The quality of our relationships determines
the quality of our lives.*
—ESTHER PEREL

In our quest to achieve greatness and leave a lasting legacy, we will need certain people in our lives to get the job done. We need people to work with us, inspire us, comfort us, and challenge us. In the same way, we want to be that person for others. A legacy is nothing if no one feels that we added value to their lives.

Steve Jobs wouldn't have created Apple without Steve Wozniak.

Napoleon was most victorious when he knew Josephine was waiting for him upon his return from battle.

Mozart could have had a longer life of composing if he had had an ally in the king's composer instead of an adversary.

Jesus's message spread across the known world because of his twelve disciples.

Les Brown grew up thinking he was mentally disabled until a teacher believed in him and gave him opportunities to learn what he was capable of.

The need for human connection is built into our being. We long for deep and meaningful connections. They inspire us and give life meaning.

However, I've observed that most of us have circles of relationships that are too small to meet all of our needs. Often we ask the key people in our lives to fill more of our needs than one person should be expected to. It's an old idea that our significant other should be everything we need, and we end up disappointed when they can't live up to that expectation.

Our society doesn't help either. We're encouraged to live as rugged individuals who don't need anyone. We live in a culture of isolation where we don't even know our neighbors. The result is that loneliness has become an epidemic—a painful condition too many live with. No matter how much we intuitively know that we need people, our egos don't want to admit it. It feels like weakness.

You may have been hurt or betrayed by people in the past. You may have lost any desire to deal with people ever again. But it's essential that you get healing, learn the lessons, and reengage because people will also be the greatest assets in your life.

The truth is that people can add value to nearly every aspect of our lives. Let's look at the entire scope of benefits we can receive from key relationships in our lives. When you list them out, it also becomes obvious where the gaps are that we need to fill.

As I thought through the list of people we need in our lives, I came up with a list of ten relationships, nine of which start with the letter "C." Some people may fill more than one of these roles, but we will be lacking if we don't find at least one source for all of these.

CARE: Some people's role is to care for you. Often this is your significant other. Although this is the most influential relationship in your life, it can either strengthen your soul or tear you down if the relationship isn't strong. In the pages ahead, I'll share with you some breakthrough ways to make this relationship mutually nurturing and deeply satisfying in what I call "Romantic Mastery." If you're single, you have to be the one to care for yourself first and find caring friends or family members to fill this role. Yes, you are 100 percent responsible for your own happiness and care, but the best relationships are with people who genuinely care for you, and you are that caring person for them. Who offers care in your life today?

COMPETENCE: Some people teach and train you to grow your skill sets. Often, this is a mentor, coworker, or class we sign up for. I took a two-year certification course with Dr. Robert Glover, but, along the way, we became friends like family. Aside from our personal friendship, my skills and core competencies grew, thus, so did my ability to add value to others. Who are you learning from?

CONSISTENCY: Some people are a regular part of your life. As much as we need adventure, we also need some people to just be there for us. It can be our family, but it can also be a friend who will always be there, take our calls, and come to our side in our hour of need. Who do you have in your life that would take your call 24/7?

CHARACTER: Some people demonstrate character and call you to rise up and live to a higher standard. My dad and mom have been these people for me. They have been married for more than sixty years. They've kept to their values all of their lives. I feel called to live to a higher standard just by their example. This role may also be people you know from anywhere you go frequently. Who do you know that demonstrates character traits you would like to emulate?

COMFORT: We need to have a safe place to share our deepest feelings and dreams. It's hard to trust people, but we need to find at least one person who is that place of comfort and acceptance for us. Who do you have in your life that cares for you unconditionally?

CONNECTION: We need people we can feel comfortable and connected with who share our values. These are the people we look forward to spending time with because they get us. When we interact with people who see the world the same way we do, we realize we are not alone. There are many like-minded people in the world. People with similar hobbies and values whom we enjoy conversations with. We don't have to agree on everything, but the interactions feel good. Even when we don't see them often we miss them. Who do you feel a connection with?

COMPANIONSHIP: Nothing fills our soul like a good friend. There are people who need to do nothing other than just be present with us and we feel refreshed. It's effortless and pleasant to spend time with a companion. Who do you have in your life that you'd think of first when you want to share an adventure or a simple dinner with?

CAREER: Some people share the journey of our work life. There are some people we only see at work. Not everyone at work encourages the best in us. Many are lazy and try to make everyone lazy so they don't feel guilty about their own work ethic. Choose your career relationships carefully and you'll continue to grow in your career and be glad you have them in your life.

CHALLENGE: We need coaches, mentors, and peers to challenge us. This is a bit different from Competence training, mentioned above. These are one-on-one relationships with people who will take a hard look at what you're doing and guide you on a path to excellence. Who motivates you to test your limits and reach higher?

INTIMACY: Sexual intimacy is a driving force for meaningful connection. The beautiful expression of intimacy is more than desire and pleasure, although it is that. It's also a deep longing to feel spiritually at home with another human being. True sexual intimacy is as much of an emotional need for connection as it is physical. How is your love life?

In our culture of the "self-made" person and push for autonomy and individuality, we run the risk of missing out on the real juice of life: soul connections. I've heard many people express their pride when they declare, "I don't need anyone." But those people won't leave a legacy as I define it, where others will talk fondly about how their lives were touched by them in a positive way.

Robert Waldinger is a psychiatrist who currently directs the Harvard Study of Adult Development, which is one of the longest-running studies on human happiness and well-being. This study has followed the lives of 724 men since 1938, including a mix of students and men from the inner city. Based on the research from this study, Dr. Waldinger comes to the following conclusion: "The clearest message that we get from this 75-year study is this: Good relationships keep us happier and healthier. Period. . . . Loneliness kills. It's as powerful as smoking or alcoholism."

He goes on to say that "people who are more socially connected to family, to friends, to the community, are happier, they're physically healthier, and they live longer than people who are less well connected."[2]

When you look at the list above, you'll see that some of these relationships are professional, or coaches you hire. But most of them are interpersonal relationships where there is a natural give and take, or as Dr. Robert Glover calls them, "cooperative/reciprocal relationships." These are very satisfying for both of you.

Relationship Value Assessment

Do a quick assessment. Take an inventory of the relationships you have now. In each of these ten areas, write down a name, or names, of people who currently fill each of these roles in your life. Leave a blank if you don't have anyone in that particular area right now:

CARE: Who offers care in your life today?

_____

_____

_____

2   Robert Waldinger, "What Makes a Good Life? Lessons from the Longest Study on Happiness," TED, December 23, 2015, https://www.ted.com/talks/robert_waldinger_what_makes_a_good_life_lessons_from_the_longest_study_on_happiness/.

COMPETENCE: Who teaches and trains you to grow your skill sets?

_____

_____

_____

CONSISTENCY: Who is a regular part of your life?

_____

_____

_____

CHARACTER: Who demonstrates character worthy of emulation?

_____

_____

_____

COMFORT: Who offers you a safe place to share your true self?

_____

_____

_____

CONNECTION: Who are the like-minded people in your life?

_____

_____

_____

COMPANIONSHIP: Who do you love spending time with socially?

_____

_____

_____

CAREER: Who shares the journey in your work life?

_____

_____

_____

CHALLENGE: Who are your coaches and mentors or those who challenge you?

_____

_____

_____

INTIMACY: Who provides you with sexual intimacy?

_____

_____

_____

Take a look at your list. Be grateful for the people who are in your life right now. Be intentional about nurturing these relationships. This exercise also shows where you need to add some key people to your life. The solution for that is simple. Go back to the blank sections and think about where you might meet people who could fill that particular need. Where do they hang out where you might have a common interest? What kinds of services or coaches would you need to hire? How can you engage and add value to these people? You'll have to initiate contact and show genuine interest, but it needs to be done. The first people you reach out to may not be the fit you're looking for, but keep searching. It's worth it. You are worth it. Take responsibility for loving yourself and filling your needs so you will live with abundance. Only from abundance can we truly serve others.

As you interact with each, how did you make them feel for having spent time with you? Make it your goal that they leave each encounter with you feeling better about themselves. I love this quote from Maya Angelou because it is the heart of your legacy: "I've learned that people will forget what you said, people will forget what you did, but people will never forget how you made them feel."

Understand this: people are the ones who determine your legacy. Your legacy is what people say to others about how you impacted their lives. It's not what you say about yourself.

Some people add value and inspiration to your life, as you do to theirs. Others sharpen you into the person you are capable of being. There is also a third group: those you may never meet but can still impact, which we'll go over in chapter 10 when we talk about how you can touch the masses through your creations. But this chapter is about those you interact with personally.

All of the great memories of my life have been shared with people. And all of the people who were with me in those moments would say the same.

There is one other principle about people I need to share with you and it's this: not everyone deserves equal amounts of your time and attention. In fact, you'll have five circles of relationships, and each will be given different time and focus priorities.

I will use the model of Jesus for this example, but it's a universal principle:

1. **Your Beloved**: I mentioned before that you need to have at least one person in the world you can share your innermost world with. It could be your spouse, but for some it's a best friend who is closer than anyone else. Jesus had John, who was called the beloved of Jesus.

2. **Your Inner Circle**: Beyond your beloved, you may have two or three who are partners, dear friends, or people who are part of your daily life in another way. This group knows you better than anyone else in the world does. You can trust them and call on them 24/7, and they know they can do the same with you. Jesus had Peter, James, and John who he shared experiences and teachings with that he didn't with the rest of the disciples or the crowds that followed him.

3. **Your Outer Circle**: Jesus had twelve disciples who were part of his team. You may have a dozen people you see regularly in your life that you enjoy spending time with. These are the ones you'd invite over if you were having a barbecue, and they'd invite you to theirs.

4. **Your Network**: You may not be aware of this, but there were 120 people who followed Jesus wherever he went. You may have about the same number of people that you see in the course of a month. You may know most of them by name, but certainly all of them by face. This is your network.

5. **The Masses**: Jesus preached to thousands of people at any one time. You may have thousands of followers on social media, or millions who saw you on a TV spot or podcast interview. Millions may read your book, see your art, admire a building you designed, or listen to music you produced. You can touch them all, yes, but not give each of them the time you'd give to your Beloved, Inner Circle, or Outer Circle.

It only makes sense to give more time and attention to nurturing your closest circle of relationships than you would with someone in the masses. Further, you will have different people rotate through your groups as situations change. It may be that you work with one group intensely for a month to launch a product, but they aren't as involved in your life a year later. Today is all you have, so look at those who deserve your time and attention now, but keep in contact with them if they move to an outer circle.

Your Children

One circle that never changes is your children. There's a lot that could be said about how to raise strong children. I do want to keep this focused on your legacy, but I'll offer two quick thoughts I resonate with deeply on the topic of raising children.

1. "Don't let your kids do anything that makes you dislike them."—Jordan B. Peterson

2. "I want to raise my children to be conscientious, autonomous, and confident."—Matthew McConaughey

At this point in my life, I have three children and four grandchildren. I'm very proud of my kids. My eldest daughter is an executive at an education software company, and her husband owns a coffee roasting company. She has three young boys who are adorable. My older son has a PhD in psychotherapy and married a woman with the same credentials. They have a private practice together and just adopted a beautiful little girl. My youngest earned a degree in video game design and is currently serving in the Air Force and is just starting his adult life.

Life has not been easy for any of them, but I'm proud they grew up and found their way. I love connecting with them as often as we can.

In terms of legacy, many people will think about their children first. They may carry your name. They may keep to the values you taught them. But have you identified what values your family stands for and made it a priority to model those in your home? Perhaps you make it a tradition that you all have dinner together. Perhaps you control the use of their phones at home. If hard work and honesty are your values, how is that showing up? Do you talk about the values in your home? When your children tell you about the stories from their day, and how other children behave, use those as teaching moments to illustrate how your family is unique and why your values are important.

Raising strong children means that they will be driven to create their own legacy as well. You may be able to leave them with assets, which we'll talk about in chapter 9, but your assets should just be a launching pad for them to do even greater things. Too many people want to make things easier for their kids than it was for them. But your struggles are what made you who you are today. You should hope they fight and struggle to do something great. Yes, your legacy should help your children to do even more than you; not have it easier than you.

Creating Emotional Bonds

My dad taught me a deep wisdom years ago. He was a career pastor for fifty years and told me this: "Son, do you know why people love their pastor? It's because he is there at the peak moments in their lives. He is there at their weddings, birth of their children, and baptisms. But he's also there at their low times: funerals, hospitalizations, and loss. Make it a priority to show up in people's lives at their peak times—the good and bad. They will remember you fondly and forever." People will bond with you in their greatest emotional moments. Just show up and be there.

I've remembered this lesson and kept it at the front of my mind. There have been times when I heard friends lost their jobs. Knowing this lesson, I made it a priority to show up at his house just to be there. Often when someone loses a loved one, people don't know how to respond. They may feel awkward and not know what to say so they stay away. Don't be like that. Just show up. Being there in those times is all that's required. They'll know that you care and they'll remember it forever.

I've spent extra time with you developing this section on people because they are the core of your legacy. People add vibrance and meaning to your life. They can lift you up and inspire you. But they are also the repository of your legacy. People will tell the stories and share the memories you create as a true legacy maker.

Now, as an exercise, let's flip the equation. Write the names of people for whom you are this person in their lives:

CARE: Who do you care for?

_____

_____

_____

COMPETENCE: Who do you train in a skill?

_____

_____

_____

CONSISTENCY: Whose life are you a consistent part of?

_____

_____

_____

CHARACTER: Who is looking at your example?

_____
_____
_____

COMFORT: Who are you a safe person to share thoughts and emotions with?

_____
_____
_____

CONNECTION: Who finds real connection with you?

_____
_____
_____

COMPANIONSHIP: Who would say you are their friend?

_____
_____
_____

CAREER: Who would say they enjoy working with you?

_____
_____
_____

CHALLENGE: Who are you mentoring?

_____
_____
_____

INTIMACY: Who are you providing a spiritual and physical bond with?

_____
_____
_____

Authenticity

Just today I was coaching a career-driven young man who had risen to be fire department captain in a well-established city years ahead of any of his predecessors. But he'd not appreciated the value of deep connections with people along the way. He'd never had a long-term romantic relationship. He had no close friendships. Those who worked with him didn't consider him as a companion, just a driven leader. He'd focused entirely on what would get him promoted in his career. Now, in a place of sad isolation, he's taking the time to reevaluate his priorities.

When your time comes to evaluate your legacy, people are the first priority. A successful legacy maker will have many people they touched who will express deep gratitude for having known them.

Developing deep connections with people starts with one thing: an intention to cultivate deeper relationships. You have to want to have people who add value to your life and whose life you add value to.

Remember, John C. Maxwell has said something to the effect of, "My definition of success is that those who know me best are also those who love me the most." Read that again. People may say they love an actor they only know based on his public image. But, as we know from social media, the things people will display to the world are only a small glimpse into the life of the real person, and typically only the most positive images. It's those who know us best who will reflect who we truly are.

True connection requires authenticity. You have to let people get to know you: how you think, what you love, and the pains you've endured. Allow people into your life. Share your thoughts, emotions, victories, and setbacks. Even little details will tell people about you. Do you love cigars, NASCAR, pets, or your church? Do the people in your life know what you love and what you believe in? I encourage you to let people into your life.

Likewise, maintain a genuine curiosity in them. There are few things that will draw you closer to a person than curiosity; when you really want to know more about them, their loves, and challenges.

It doesn't take a lot of extra effort; just a desire to understand the person in front of you, and to let them into your world. That's authenticity.

One last word on deepening your relationships is to stop time and value key moments. What do I mean by that? It occurred to me that some of my deepest relationship memories were the quiet moments, just sitting with a friend and taking in the beauty of a moment. It may come after we've connected in good conversation and shared a good feeling. Then we just sit and bask in the energy of the moment, often in silence, and take everything in. Notice where you are and what's around you. How you're feeling at that moment. I remember sitting on a bench overlooking the Amazon River with my local boat driver after he took me to his village to meet his family. I shared with him one of the cigars I brought. We quietly took in the majestic scene in front of us. It was powerful. I've had moments like this in romance, adventures, and even just sitting on my back porch with a friend. Value the quiet moments shared. They can be the deepest and most meaningful of your life.

Romantic Mastery

There is one relationship that is more important than all others and will impact your emotions, productivity, and overall quality of life, and that's the one you pick to share your life with—your spouse or significant other. Picking the right partner is critical, but just as important is how to maintain the relationship so it serves and nurtures both of you. You get married because you fall deeply in love. We all love those emotions. Truly, the honeymoon emotions are some of the greatest we can experience in this world.

But what happens that causes people to lose those feelings? Why do so many marriages fail or create roommate-like relationships over time? In many of my live talks, I've asked the audience to answer this question: "How many relationships do you know that are so beautiful you would even envy what they have?" Do you know a couple who are tender and cute together? Perhaps they are touching each other continually and seem to genuinely enjoy each other deeply. On average, 65 percent of people I surveyed could only identify one couple they knew like that. For many, that number was zero. What are your chances of being one of those couples others would envy if you don't even have the good role models to emulate?

For more than a decade I ran an international matchmaking business that introduced many couples to each other, and more than 450 of these couples eventually married. We learned so much along the way. Our dedication was to help these couples succeed, more than just introduce them to each other. The results of our efforts were remarkable. As we kept in touch with our couples, we realized that more than 90 percent were still married after our eleven years in business.

In order for you to have a better chance at staying in love, you need a better model than the one you've been taught all of your life. You need to understand why these others aren't working.

The most common thought is that relationships should be a fifty-fifty proposition, meaning that each gives equally to the relationship. The problem with this is that neither gives exactly half at any point in time. If one is deep in a project, there is a chance the other may feel a bit left out if they are measuring by this fifty-fifty model. You often hear people complaining that they are doing all of the work in the relationship. The common solution is to seek out relationship counseling. The goal of most of these counselors is to make both parties feel heard and arrive at a negotiation to make the unhappy partner more satisfied. Even if the couple can arrive at terms for moving forward, there will always come a point in time when a deal point doesn't get met. Fights return and misery along with it. Are relationships really supposed to be "negotiated" like business deals? Where's the romance in that?

Others think it should be 100/100, meaning that you give everything you have whether the other person reciprocates or not. Even if this approach works in the honeymoon stage, it almost certainly guarantees that one party will be doing more than the other at some point and leave the other feeling unappreciated.

Very briefly, I will share with you the three keys to staying in deep romantic love with the one you share life with.

1. Celebrate Your Uniqueness

"Well, that's the way my parents did it when I was growing up!" Have you heard that before, or felt it yourself in one form or another? You're not the only one. It's human nature to carry our beliefs and identities with us where we go, even if they don't serve us. Many of those identities were molded into us in childhood when we didn't have the cognitive ability to evaluate them and decide whether they were right for us. In truth, we don't know where most of our beliefs originated, but we cling to them with our lives!

When people try to impose their beliefs about how their relationship *should* go, they are already setting up separation with the person they love without knowing it.

The very best thing any couple can do, when they are in the honeymoon stage, is to talk with each other about what they love about who they uniquely are together. Do you love the sense of humor you share? Maybe the things you have in common that connect you—things you both love doing together. In those early stages, many couples adopt their own vocabulary to describe how they are with each other. Some have inside jokes. Others have already developed special traditions or dates they like to go on. Capture these. Write them down.

You are not your parents, and your partner is not like theirs. When you first come together, think of it as a clean slate, a new beginning to something wonderful that you want to hold on to and cherish.

The value of doing this in the honeymoon stage is that you can set an emotional marker, a standard, of what your relationship is like at its best. When you both see it clearly, you can hold it easier. It creates a standard to measure how you are with each other at any time.

When you get into a disagreement, you understand the purpose of the conflict is to resolve it, and remove anything that has taken you out of that peak state of love and tenderness, so you can return to it as quickly as possible. Some see disagreements as a battlefield, and a contest to win, and the very purpose of the relationship is lost in the conflict, egos, and emotions.

What is the purpose of your romantic relationship? Romance! Don't you want to feel like a teenager in love every day of your life? Talk about it with your partner. If you both agree that you want to be in love and stay in love, then that goal will influence how you are with each other in everything. But that is the primary goal: mutual agreement to be in and stay in romantic love.

If your relationship has grown stale, have the conversation with your partner in this way. Share with them that your heart wants to be in love and feel love with them. That's why you picked them. See whether they want to feel that way with you again too. Get back on the same page and make tender emotions and affection your goal. Then, when you are not feeling those feelings, you can pause for a moment to ask each other what happened that took you out of those tender emotions and what you can do now to get back to love.

Hold the standard of being in honeymoon love as your purpose and priority for being in the relationship and keep it there. If you both share this clear intention, you can have love and romance to last your life.

2. Understand That Two Are Now One

One of the things that breaks my heart is to see couples fight in public. You can feel the egos flare up as they use a public audience as a way to show the other how wrong they are. It's painful for everyone in the room, and a complete disservice to the relationship.

One of the things I learned clearly from living abroad for so many years is that many cultures value their families and honor them in front of everyone, even at times when they are privately in conflict. No matter how things are going at home, they will praise their spouse publicly in respect for the relationship.

As I tried to understand what made the difference in their views, I started to hear common descriptions in how they described their relationships. In the West, we talk about our spouse as our life partner. Overseas, they say that their partner is their other half. As I dug further into this, I understood what they were talking about. According to Greek mythology, humans originally had two heads, four arms, and four legs. Zeus feared that they were becoming too powerful, so he split them into two separate beings and separated them from one side of the earth to the other. Now, according to the story, they spend their lives searching to be reunited with their other half.

Many other cultures identify themselves with their social circles and family as part of who they are. Here in the US, we tend to see ourselves as autonomous individuals. One woman explained to me that she always goes out looking good because she wouldn't want one of her mother's friends to see her looking sloppy and tell her about it. It would be disrespectful. She wants her mother to only hear good things about how she treated people and carried herself. She represents her mother for how she was raised, even as a young adult.

Even more, they really see their spouses as an extension of themselves. As I was explaining how I'd seen couples fight in public in the United States to a married woman in Ukraine she declared, "I'd never do that! Why would I want to hurt myself that way?" Hurt yourself? She truly saw that publicly hurting her man was the same as hurting herself. Wow. What a different perspective!

Have you ever thought about your spouse as an extension of you? Do you want them to be proud of you wherever you are? When you see them in this light, it changes how you see the relationship. In many ways, your life is a reflection of how well you connect with your significant other. That they represent you, and you represent them. You are each a mirror of how well you care for each other and you each want the other to be happy you chose each other.

This concept goes back thousands of years when these words were first written in the book of Genesis, and I paraphrase, "And for this reason they shall leave their mother and father and the two shall become one."

You are now one functioning entity in many regards. If you both see it this way, you'll find greater harmony and mutual love and respect and compassion. The two of you have become one.

3. Fill Each Other's Cups

I was having lunch with a colleague of mine who had lived in Japan for three years. He invited me to a traditional Japanese restaurant and told me about a tradition they have. "In Japan, the bottles of water, beer, or sake on the table are poured into the glasses by those at the table, not the waitress or waiter," he explained. "But you don't serve yourself, just your guests as their cups become empty, and they will fill yours." It sounded simple enough, but as we were thirty minutes into our lunch, I suddenly realized that my friend's glasses were empty! I quickly apologized and refilled his water and beer glasses. He was gracious and not offended. But I will tell you one thing for sure, the rest of that meal I was keenly aware of the status of his drinks!

It occurred to me how beautiful of an illustration this is for healthy relationships. What if both of you took responsibility for making sure your partner's glasses were filled?

First, you'd have to both want to make sure the other knows you care and want to fill their cups for them if they need it. In healthy relationships, both know what their cups are and are perfectly capable of filling them on their own. But there is a magical spark of love when someone knows us and wants to make sure we are happy. They can sense when one of our cups is running low and will offer to fill a cup from time to time.

Second, you will need to learn what their cups are! Do you know what makes your partner happy? Can you tell when they're bored or needing affection? Do you see times when you could offer to help them with something they're doing? And, yes, you can ask if they need sex if you haven't been together in a while. Learn their "happy places." These are places they go that just improve their mood, or things they do that are enjoyable like reading a book, or encouraging them to spend some time with one of their good friends. Encourage them to seek these out if they feel down.

Finally, check in with them from time to time on how their cups are doing since many of us hide behind "I'm fine," even to our significant others.

These three tips represent the difference between settling into roommate status and keeping the honeymoon emotions alive and well. Remember, this relationship will influence every part of your life so make it a joy. Be in love like teenagers always. It is more than possible.

In Conclusion

In study after study, one of the greatest indicators of a happy life, and even the lengthening of our days, is the quality of the relationships we have with people.

1. Have circles of people that fill all of the "Cs" in your life

2. Make sure you are that person's or someone else's "C" in their lives

3. Go deeper with relationships that are close to you

4. Stay in love with the one you chose to be your partner

This alone will make for a richly satisfying life, and you will be fondly remembered by many.

While building your legacy, you can create relationships where people will carry fond memories from having been connected to you in one way or another. It is more in your control than you may have realized. But it will also be very satisfying while you are living out your legacy today.

When I finished writing the introduction to this book, where I first told the story of Rick and his legacy, I decided to share it with his daughter, Rachel. I thought she should see it before the world does. Her response was so beautiful and touching. She wrote to me, "I keep having to stop because it's making me so emotional. It's so beautiful, Marcum. I'm having to read through eyes filled with tears. It's so well written. My dad would have loved this. It's so funny. Just this morning I wrote down 'Leave a Legacy' in the little book I do with my daughter too." Now I'm tearing up. This is just another example of the joy we can find in connecting with people and discovering the riches in relationships.

If you need more resources and inspiration to help you build and deepen relationships, visit MarcumDavis.com/Legacy.

The next chapter is a favorite topic of mine: Experiences! There is nothing like a great experience to create lasting memories and deepen relationships.

Chapter 8:

Experiences: We Are the Sum of Our Stories

The purpose of life is to live it, to taste experiences to the utmost, to reach out eagerly and without fear for newer and richer experiences.
—ELEANOR ROOSEVELT

I was raised as a child of the 1970s—from age seven to seventeen. It was a glorious time to be a kid. No cell phones, internet, or personal computers. Video games were just being invented. The world felt safer. Mom would let me ride my bike to my friend's house to hang out and play with the simple instructions "Just be home for dinner."

As a pastor, my dad would regularly have people over for dinner at our home after church on Sundays. It was often very interesting to sit at the table and listen in on the conversations. At that time, we still had many veterans from World War II who were alive and would share stories of their valiant deeds and heroics. Others would share stories of their lives in the 1950s when they started their families and businesses and life felt magical. Just as the popular TV series was titled, those were the "Happy Days" for many of that generation.

After a period of time, however, I noticed a trend. Most of these stories were from twenty years prior, or more! I thought, *Haven't they done anything since?* I may have only been twelve or thirteen at the time, but I vowed that I wanted the stories that I would share to be no more than six months old. I wanted to always be doing something story-worthy.

However, I ended up living a very domestic life into my thirties. I hadn't been out of the country since my dad's Holy Land trip when I was eighteen. And, just like those I'd observed, I hadn't done much worth talking about in twenty years either!

I married Helen at age twenty-eight. She was a young attorney but developed a debilitating schizophrenia a few years into our marriage. I spent most of my thirties taking care of her. She would later pass away. I went into a depression. This was not the life I'd imagined for myself, at all.

The depression lasted eight grueling months. It felt like an eternity, but I was given good counsel on how to live with it. Dr. Michael Philips was my counselor and became a good friend. He explained to me that this was a "life depression," as he called it. Everything I'd told myself as a child that my life would be like didn't happen. My soul was experiencing the "death of a dream." As he counseled me, I made sure I spent time after work with some friends three or four evenings each week. I didn't do anything crazy to try to escape the pain, but I cared for myself as best I could and allowed the inner mourning process to run its course.

Then, it happened. I awoke one morning and the dark night of my soul had been completely lifted. The internal mourning was finished. I describe it like pushing down the lever on a toaster and it stayed down for eight months, but it just suddenly popped up! I was free! The feeling was exhilarating! A rush of joy filled my being. Wow! I had forgotten what it felt like to feel happy and I was elated!

My first thought was that I had been given a new chance at life. I wanted to experience everything I could and truly enjoy life! I immediately went out and bought a Mercedes convertible. Prior to that I'd only driven minivans or family sedans.

Just like Jim Carrey in the movie *Yes Man*, I started on my quest to say yes to opportunities as they came. I was invited to join the executive fishing retreat with the board of directors of the company I represented because my sales had been strong. But their idea of a fishing retreat was on the Amazon River in Brazil! *Maybe I pushed this "yes" thing too far*, I thought. But, once the fear subsided, it turned out to be amazing beyond words!

I would go on to travel to more than twenty countries across four continents. I would tour castles in Germany, visit the king's palace in Bangkok, and run zip lines in Costa Rica, among other experiences. I went back on a second trip to the Amazon River and went hunting for caiman (relative to the alligator) with the natives at night. I was proud of the photo I had holding a six-foot-long caiman in the boat.

On most of these trips, I went with a group of people and created memories for a lifetime. I recently reconnected with one of the men, a urologist from Houston, from my 2006 trip to Costa Rica. He loved me and the trip as much as I did. While I was on the phone with him, he called over others in the room to tell them who I was and showed them photos from our trip. Even though we hadn't spoken in years, it was like no time had passed at all. I knew I had a friend for life.

It was then that I realized how powerful experiences are in creating our legacies. People will talk about what they did with me for the rest of their lives as well as I would them. Even beyond the goal of creating a legacy, these experiences are some of the greatest things we can do for ourselves! You come away enriched and full of life. I wish this for you with all of my heart.

There are three principles for creating great experiences that will add to your legacy:

1. Be intentional about looking for opportunities

2. Make them adventurous

3. Do it with others

Be Intentional about Looking for Opportunities

The problem with ruts is that it takes effort to step out of them! Deep trenches are created from our daily routines. If you aren't intentional, you'll stay in them and never have adventures. How long has it been since you did something story-worthy? Our life may be the sum of our stories, but you won't find good stories in the drudgery of sameness. It takes effort and forethought to break routines and realize how our comfort zones have us trapped in a storyless existence.

I encourage you to create a mental marker for yourself, like a red flag, if you've gone too long since your last adventure. Start looking for opportunities to break out and do something new and different. How long has it been since you did something worth telling a story about? As I mentioned earlier, I made it a goal to not allow six months to go by without having tried something or done something new that was story-worthy. But it doesn't happen by accident.

A man once had a dream of winning the lottery. He prayed to God every day, "Please let me win the lottery today!" Finally, after years of these prayers, God answered him, "Can you at least meet me halfway and buy a lottery ticket?"

Finding opportunities for great experiences may be easier and simpler than you might think. When I first opened myself up to wanting to add experiences to my life, I found that it was more of a matter of my willingness to say "yes" to opportunities as they came up. When I was in my twenties, I remember a family in our church inviting us to come join them on an RV camping trip. All I had to do was come up with $200 so they could rent the larger RV to accommodate all of us. I thought about the disruption of my work schedule and a few other excuses that prompted me to decline. But as soon as I hung up the phone from saying no, I regretted it. It would have been great. We loved their family and weren't doing anything that would have prevented it. I would have had great memories for my entire family. What memories do I have from saving the money and spending a few more days at work? In retrospect, I was doing very little for my young family at that time, with regard to going on vacations or anything else. I was filled with excuses and fears that were pathetic.

Once I decided that experiences were an important priority to me, I started saying yes, including to some scary invitations, like fishing on the Amazon River! It didn't take long to feel the vibrancy for life in these experiences before I started seeking them out. Now, if I go even two months without at least traveling somewhere to visit a friend, I feel the itch.

What types of experiences can you look for? Start with thinking about the experiences of the past that you loved and where you created memories with others. Was it a camping trip, fishing trip, retreat, or bike ride? Often our grand experiences involve travel. But they can also be as simple as a night on the town with friends, dinner or drinks at a favorite restaurant, or going to a concert. Mix it up and keep adding them to your calendar, regularly.

We will always make time and effort and find the money to do the things we have decided are important to us. Decide to make new experiences a normal and important part of your life.

Make Them Adventurous

Most anything that takes us out of the norms of life will feel adventurous. But the excuses will seem real as well. You may genuinely be pressed for time. You may have financial constraints. Your spouse or kids may have schedules to consider. But the regret of living a life of no adventures is worse, much worse. You'll be amazed to see how many of these details suddenly work themselves out once you've made a true decision to do something. The moment you start looking at calendars and putting the money together, everything else starts to come into alignment with your wishes.

But what makes for adventurous experiences? I find there are three aspects to adventure:

- Trying something new
- Going somewhere new
- Stretching to new challenges

Trying Something New may be as simple as learning to play an instrument, climbing a rock wall, learning a new language, taking dance classes, or just going to a restaurant you've heard about. Perhaps it's as simple as wine tasting or as big as going on a safari, taking an Alaskan cruise, or doing an Ironman event. There's probably at least one thing that immediately came to your mind just now. What's kept you from starting? Most of these have great ways to make the experience even more of an adventure by doing them with a group or traveling to a conference with others who have the same interests as you.

Even if you're going someplace you've gone before, do something to make it new this time. If you go to New York, hire one of those bicycle taxis and tell the driver you'll give them a bonus tip if they'll get you there fast and race with your companions in their bike taxis! Let the adventure begin!

I didn't grow up fishing, but I became hooked on adventure fishing. I've gone sailfishing off the coast of Costa Rica, tuna fishing in Monterey, walleye fishing in Canada, in addition to peacock bass fishing on the Amazon River. I hadn't done any of these before I was forty-two, but I have loved every trip since. It's never too late to start!

Going Somewhere New is one of my favorite things to do. When I first went on that Amazon River fishing trip, it was the first time I'd been outside of the US in twenty-two years. Everything was larger than life and filled my senses. But one of the great side benefits for me was a new love of anything new. I became fascinated just traveling to another city. My senses became alive with fascination and curiosity. How do these people live differently? I looked at the scenery with a fresh appreciation. Once you see all of life with eyes of wonder, you'll never lack a sense of adventure again.

When I got to visit Bangkok on business, every moment was filled with sights and sounds that captivated me. On my third trip there, I reasoned that I'd already covered the expenses for travel there, so what else could I do? I took the short flight to Phuket and spent extra days going around the islands in places I'd only seen in travel videos. It only cost a few hundred dollars more, but it created even more excitement and lasting memories.

Since I started traveling at age forty-two, I've now been to more than twenty new countries. I wish this kind of adventure for everyone. You'll come back changed and filled with a new life energy you didn't know existed before.

Stretching to New Challenges may sound simple, or a bit scary, but we need to be challenged if we want to grow. Our modern Western culture seems to value laziness and self-indulgence over challenge in a way that isn't benefiting us. You've seen how many people just work to get to the weekend. We even have a popular restaurant chain called TGI Fridays, meaning Thank God It's Friday. Why do so many millions live for the weekends? Perhaps it's because they want to relax and be removed from the challenges of work—to unwind. So what value do we give to the vast majority of our days? Many see Mondays through Fridays as necessary inconveniences to get to the weekends of leisure and escape. But is that a fulfilling way to live?

Additionally, most seem to long for the day when they can retire. Why? Because they think there will come a day when they won't have any struggles; a day that will never come, even with financial independence. And what is the result of making this our ultimate goal as a culture? We work our entire lives in hopes of one day doing nothing. Seriously. Where is the adventure in that?

And the results are alarming. The biblical warning that people without a vision perish is very real. On average, people only live a few years after they retire. It's like they have told themselves that their days of usefulness are done and their bodies begin to comply. One classic study followed a group of people who retired between ages sixty-two and sixty-five and showed that the majority died within three to five years.[3]

People who only work for the weekends also seem to complain about their work in epidemic fashion and treat their jobs with contempt. I had the privilege of living in Ukraine for many years and witnessed the difference in work ethic to those in the US firsthand. A young Ukrainian man I met was a translator for the military. He was the liaison for foreign countries who brought support. He explained it this way: "I finally understood the difference in how you see the world. In the West, you expect life to be good and when it isn't, you can't stand it, and fight to change it right away. In Ukraine, we see life as hard and when it's good we celebrate!"

To have an expectation that life should be easy and complain at every difficulty and discomfort is shortsighted. It's the struggle that makes us great and creates the great stories we value most! When it is good, fantastic! Celebrate! When times are tough, don't become discouraged because of unrealistic expectations. Roll with it. I found some wisdom in their perspective.

---

3   S. G. Haynes, A. J. McMichael, and H. A. Tyroler, "Survival after Early and Normal Retirement," *Journal of Gerontology* 33, no. 2 (March 1, 1978): 269–78, https://doi.org/10.1093/geronj/33.2.269.

Do you remember the first time you heard about the dangers of our "comfort zones"? I sure do. I realized how much my primary drive had been for comfort and the end result would be a life of no change, stagnation, and drudgery. But getting out of my comfort zone meant being uncomfortable and being stretched to do things I hadn't done before and would certainly not be good at first. It would mean learning new things and even risking looking ignorant in the beginning. But I quickly realized that if I wasn't feeling uncomfortable by being stretched, then it meant I wasn't growing or doing anything new either. I developed an internal red flag to too much comfort. It meant to me that I'd stagnated and needed a new adventure to stretch me again.

When you're looking at experiences to add to your life, consider things you may have shied away from in the past because of fears of the unknown or discomfort. Change your mindset to embrace those as your new norm. They are the source of growth, progress, and proof that you're living your life to the fullest! Without challenge and adventure, what do you have? Sounds like a very boring life to me.

What are you doing now that is stretching you? Create a list of great adventures you'd like to add in the near future and others to put on your bucket list. Include things that might scare you today, but that you could do if you applied yourself. I mean this exercise literally. Make the time to do it now. I've found that what I put down on paper I've eventually accomplished, even if it was decades later. Dream big. Stretch yourself. This is where the juice of life lives.

Do It with Others

I spent five years of my thirties as an architectural representative for a division of US Brick. Our specialty was creating themed environments with historic brick aesthetics, such as restaurants or stores that added stone to their construction designs. Two of my grandest projects were the New York-New York Hotel & Casino in Las Vegas and the GameWorks emporiums, a joint venture with Steven Spielberg, Sega, and Universal Studios.

The job fed my ego and my belly with stays at luxury hotels across the nine western states including a personal daily food budget for fine dining. As a younger man in his thirties, I felt like hot stuff wearing suits to architectural presentations and being the product expert on construction sites. The glow of this lifestyle was euphoric for the first couple of years. However, if you've ever traveled alone as extensively as I did, you know how empty it becomes after a while.

I'll never forget one particular evening when I was reclining poolside at a Long Beach, California, resort with a glass of red wine in one hand and a cigar in the other. As I watched the sun go down over the Pacific Ocean, it was like a scene from a movie. It was breathtaking. At that moment, I turned my head to the left to tell someone next to me, "Isn't this amazing?" But I stopped mid-sentence to realize that there was no one there. I was completely alone. The weight of the heavy silence crushed my heart. I felt even more alone. There was no one to share this with.

Many other young men my age had envied my job and couldn't possibly understand why I wanted to leave it. I'd explain it this way: "Imagine that you get to have a day at Disneyland—all by yourself. It was just like that. What's the point? It's worse than not going at all." Once I began to really travel in my forties, I made it a priority to go with people, and the more people, the better! So I did. There is nothing that compares with shared experiences with other people, even if you didn't know them before you arrived.

This is one of the reasons why people go to conferences and conventions. You could just stay home and take the courses online and get the same information, couldn't you? Of course you could. But the vibrational energy of being with other like-minded people ignites your soul. Don't go alone.

Even if the experience is just a vacation with family or friends, it presents opportunities for adventure. In fact, it might not surprise you to learn that families who have fun together and participate in activities that are interesting to everyone can develop strong bonds that last a lifetime.

Camping trips, hiking, and other fun activities can be a great way for families to connect and create shared memories.

Do you have stories from camping trips you can recall? Perhaps the bear ate all of the food or you were caught in a downpour. As wild as it may sound, adventures are the things we relish most. They are story-worthy.

Making your experiences into adventures doesn't mean you have to scale El Capitan with rock climbing equipment, although that does sound cool. Creating new adventures can be as simple as going to a theme park or on a camping trip with friends or family. Most times, the adventure finds you in the experience. But no adventure happens without going. My encouragement is that you make it a priority to go with people.

Experiences That Create Family Memories

Creating experiences with our families can bond us closer together and become stories our kids will share with their children one day. I would be doing my dad a disservice if I didn't mention an incredible experience he created for our family.

I am the eldest of three sons. As a pastor and his wife, my dad and mom made our family a priority. I'm sure they were motivated to be an example to others in the church, but we always felt that family was important to them. What I'll share now is a very uncommon story. I've never heard another like it.

As part of the Los Gatos Christian Church, with church attendance well over five thousand each week, my dad was head of a large staff. It operated like many of the other Silicon Valley businesses in the area, meaning he only had two or three weeks of personal vacation time each year. When I was twelve, he made the decision to save up his vacation time for a couple of years until he had accumulated six weeks. He was a meticulous planner and charted a trip for us that would take us around thirty-three states of the country to see many of the historic sites and natural wonders in the United States—all with paper maps.

Starting from San Jose, California, my dad, mom, brothers, and I all piled into our Town & Country station wagon and drove off. It would be difficult to truly describe how amazing the trip was. We saw so many places of beauty including the Grand Canyon, Carlsbad Caverns, Niagara Falls, Devils Tower, the Grand Tetons, and many more. We explored American Civil War battle sites. We spent time visiting historic New England and Revolutionary War locations. We even stayed at a hotel that claimed that George Washington had slept there, and we toured Monticello, the home of Thomas Jefferson. The list goes on.

I hope this chapter has motivated you to make experiences a priority in your life. I hope it's inspired your imagination. Adventure is not an option; it's a way of life. It's a way of showing gratitude to our Creator for everything he's made available to us. Life is meant to be experienced fully. It keeps us in a state of play and childlike wonder. The alternative is boredom and sameness. Creating stories you can share takes intention, but it's worth whatever it takes to make them happen. Just be sure to bring people along for the ride.

If you need more resources and inspiration to help you create memorable and impactful experiences, visit MarcumDavis.com/Legacy.

Chapter 9:

Assets: The Currency of Dreams

Money is only a tool. It will take you wherever you wish,
but it will not replace you as the driver.
—AYN RAND

What dreams do you have? Maybe your goal is purchasing your first house, owning a sports car, or paying for your kids' college education. Perhaps you're ready to build an empire, establish a foundation, or create a multigenerational wealth plan. You may dream of financial independence—that status in life where you can follow your passions and desires because they bring fulfillment, not because you need them to pay your bills. No matter what you desire, money is the currency to bring them to life in this world.

As a legacy maker, creating assets to fuel your dreams and pass on an inheritance to your heirs is an essential part of the PEACE Legacy Formula.

Prior to reading this book, you may have thought that legacies were only about assets that were passed down to the next generation. You now know that it's only one of the five aspects of the PEACE Legacy Formula, but it's an important one. You can live with financial peace of mind and the abundance to bring the desires of your heart to life. I wish this for you passionately.

In this chapter, I want to provide value here for you, no matter what stage you're at today. You may be struggling to get out of debt, already creating passive income, growing a business, or building a multigenerational wealth plan. I just know that the deep desires in your heart were given to you for a reason. You deserve to see them realized in your lifetime as you live with a sense of deep satisfaction. I also believe that all the funding needed to bring your dreams to life is also available to you if you move forward with a plan and apply the discipline and work required.

I must confess, I don't consider myself to be an authority on money or financial planning. I've made and lost money. I don't have training specific to financial education. But I can say one thing: I've always seemed to attract money into my life, even after setbacks.

In preparation for this chapter, I attended workshops on financial basics and long-term planning. I interviewed a few of the top multigenerational asset managers in the country. But most importantly, I researched to learn where most people are with their financial goals and what they need at each stage.

Since this topic is so important to all our lives, I have pored over ideas and rewritten this chapter several times from scratch. There is so much to be said and so little amount of space to cover it all in one chapter, so I've added resources on the website to help. You'll find everything at Marcum-Davis.com/Legacy.

I condensed everything down to what I felt was most important to include in this chapter:

1. Money Mindsets
2. The Path to Freedom
3. Financial Abundance for Generations
4. Business Funding Basics

Money Mindsets

Removing Limitations

You can only go as far as you truly believe you can. Translation: *you* are the biggest reason you aren't closer to achieving the dreams in your heart.

What do you tell yourself about financial achievement?

- No one in my family has made much money. It's my lot in life.
- I have no idea how I could do any more than I'm doing now.
- I'm bad with money.
- Nothing I do seems to work.
- If I got more, I'd probably just blow it.

The millionaires who started with nothing, made it, and lost it, and made it again have this internal confidence that "I can always make more." They create a standard for themselves and work until they achieve it. They also understand that they are the source of their money, not the economy or any other factor.

Imagine this fantasy story for a moment. You and a billionaire passed by each other on a drizzly day and happened to step in the same puddle when lightning struck and the billionaire's consciousness entered your brain. You decide to let him take charge and watch to see what he would do. He's now going to work with your body and identity. Do you have any doubt that he could still create millions of dollars operating from within your world? Of course not. He knows how to do it. So why couldn't you? You are not limited. You just need to learn more and try more and then learn and try again. What you could do is hundreds of times greater than your self-limiting beliefs.

Don't let your self-talk cause you to believe you have limits. There will be enough other challenges to success. You shouldn't be one of them.

Willingness to Risk

Ever since I read that account of the regrets of those in their nineties who said they wished that they had risked more, I've been on a quest to explore the dreams that come to me before categorically dismissing them without trying.

Napoleon Hill once said, "What the mind of man can conceive and believe, it can achieve." With doubts removed, the task is to get crystal clear about what the vision looks like and then calculate what actions, resources, relationships, and funding would be required to make it a reality. If you truly do that work, the only question that remains is your willingness to pay the price to make it happen.

What are the answers to your fears of risk?

- What if I don't make it happen?
  - » How will you live with yourself if you don't try?
  - » Realize that most successes come from the process of working the plan and most outcomes have little resemblance to the original plan. Keep moving forward.
  - » Your only risk is that you don't pay attention to what the path is teaching you or that you quit trying.
- What if I'm embarrassed for failing?
  - » It's your life and there is no embarrassment in fighting for your dreams.
  - » Ditch the concern of what others will think. They aren't showing up to pay your bills or make your dreams come true.
  - » Memorize Theodore Roosevelt's famous "Man in the Arena" speech and recite it to yourself every morning.
- What if I lose money?
  - » You need to understand that every great person who has accomplished anything has both made and lost money.
  - » Decide that you will walk in the path of greatness.

» Know that you can make it again even faster after learning the lessons from this attempt.

Taking Losses in Stride

Setbacks are part of the path forward. Only you can allow them to take you off course. When you experience a true challenge, find the inner boldness to declare, "At last a worthy challenge!" You are up for it. Failure is not final. You've survived everything that's come your way up to this point in time, and you'll survive any losses of today. You've got a lot of life ahead of you. Being the "Man in the Arena" is what life is all about. You come fully alive in the quest for something deeply meaningful to you, a worthwhile endeavor. Live! Life is as much in the losses as the gains. To paraphrase Bon Jovi from his classic song, it's your life. It's now or never. You won't live forever. I just wish for you to live while you're alive because this is your life.

Take Massive Action

The true advantage you have over others is your willingness to do the work necessary to build your dream. Nothing takes the place of hard work. Education, privilege, and resources can be beaten by the one who applies oneself to the work and grind of creating success. Doing the work is a matter of discipline. Do what needs to be done, when it needs to be done, whether you feel like it or not in the moment.

Be proud of yourself that you're willing to do what others are not so you will always have what others will not.

With money mindsets in place, let's add some practical steps for building your assets.

The Path to Freedom

Let's lay out a very simple way to look at what I call the Legacy Asset Plan. Starting from the bottom and working your way up, here are the five stages of your journey:

1. **Lack:** Not enough income to pay the bills

2. **Surplus:** Income covers your bills and then some
3. **Cash Cushion:** You have six months of monthly bills set aside
4. **Independence:** Passive income now exceeds your bills
5. **Lifestyle:** Your passive income can pay for luxuries

Stage 1: Lack: Not Enough Income to Pay the Bills

If there's one thing I want you to remember about financial responsibility, it's that the reason many people don't win is because they try to live at the level of their peers rather than living below their means. And most people in this situation are filling the gaps with credit card debt at alarming rates, financing an unsustainable lifestyle.

If you find yourself in this group, don't be discouraged. In fact, don't allow your emotions to enter the equation at all. You need to take pragmatic steps, as if you were helping a good friend to get back on their feet. You should be that friend to yourself.

If you aren't bringing in enough money to cover your current spending, you have two options: reduce the bills or increase your income (or both).

To increase income, you have career options and side hustles to consider. In your career, you could look for a higher paying job, or find ways to earn more at your current job. You could also start a side hustle. There are many income opportunities you can investigate, and many people have turned those into big businesses over time. A simple Google or AI search can give you lists of opportunities that can grow from side hustles to full-time businesses. Start researching and find one that sparks something in you.

It won't take long to get to the next level, Surplus. Be proud of yourself and celebrate your milestones. You have the basic tools in place that can take you far. It will reduce stress and give you hope for a bright future. You're ready. Let's talk about life with surplus!

Stage 2: Surplus: Income Covers Your Bills and Then Some

I hope you arrive at this stage early in your life. But, even if you don't, I know I've experienced ups and downs at various times. The good news is that once you've learned how to get here, you know how to make it back again. Remember, *you* are the money source. You are the one who knows how to make it. The value is in your ability to earn, keep, and grow what you make. Keep investing in yourself. What you learn can't be taken from you.

What does surplus look like? It means you are covering all your bills with your income from your job and/or side hustle. Your next step is to set aside 10 percent of your income to begin buying passive income sources. These can come in the form of rental homes, stocks, and even forms of creations such as book royalties or online courses. Again, a simple Google or AI search for passive income ideas will provide plenty of inspiration.

It may be the first time you've experienced surplus. But don't stop here. Keep your spending in check and build a cash cushion from your surplus so you can accomplish the goal of reaching stage three, Cash Cushion.

Stage 3: Cash Cushion: You have Six Months of Monthly Bills Set Aside

Congratulations again! You've completed stage two, and you now have more income than expenses! But what to do with the surplus? It seems that most people spend it as fast as they make it and end up broke, just at a higher income. But, if you want to make your future-self love you even more, set your goal to get all the way to stage five of the Legacy Asset Plan.

Cash cushions have two benefits: insulation from financial setbacks and the ability to put more into your passive income vehicles. The goal here is to save up the equivalent total of your monthly bills times six and have it available. That number may sound big right now, but you can get there.

Without a cushion, you could be devastated by a setback, such as a job loss, and face serious consequences, like downsizing your home and car to survive. On the other side of the equation, you'll need to have these resources when you're ready to start buying sources of passive income.

It's essential to be saving aggressively now and not spending more!

What is "passive income"? Passive income is money you make that doesn't require you to personally exchange your time for it. If you owned a house that you could rent for $2,000 per month, and it costs you $1,500 in mortgage and other expenses, then you have $500 of regular passive income coming to you every month. We'll cover this more in stage four. For now, make it your goal to look at your surplus, not as a reason to buy a more expensive car or house for yourself yet, but to save up to buy more sources of passive income so that money can buy your new car when you get to stage five.

How quickly can you get to having six months of liabilities in a savings account? Do the math and get excited with each deposit you make. You're on track!

Stage 4: Independence: Passive Income Now Exceeds Your Bills

In the previous example of a rental property, where you were earning $500 per month in passive income, you might rightfully conclude that it isn't enough to cover your bills. No, but you can see that it has put you on the right track. You just need to do more.

The good news is that the next one will come faster! How? Because now you have $500 more to add to your cushion account than you did before. Additionally, that rental house is continuing to grow in value, as is your personal residence. It may take half as long to have the money you'll need to buy the next passive income asset.

Homes aren't the only way to create passive income, and it's wise to diversify income sources so you don't rely entirely on real estate for passive income in case we experience another real estate crash. Here are some other ideas for you to consider:

1. **Dividend-paying investments:** Income generated through ownership of stocks, mutual funds, or exchange-traded funds (ETFs) that pay regular dividends.

2. **Royalties:** Income earned from creative works, such as books, music, patents, or trademarks.

3. **Online businesses:** Earnings generated from online ventures, such as e-commerce stores, digital products, or online courses.

No matter which forms of passive income you pick, make it your ambition to become highly knowledgeable in that arena. Take courses. Hire advisors and consultants. But, at the end of the day, it's your money and your future. You are the one who needs to know what you're doing.

Stage 4's goal is financial independence, meaning your passive income grows to exceed your monthly bills so you could drop your day job if you decided to.

You just bought your freedom.

Stage 5: Lifestyle: Your Passive Income Can Pay for Luxuries

This is the stuff of dreams. Your passive income businesses continue to grow and can now pay for the car of your dreams, the house of your dreams, and the cost of travel to places of your dreams. How? Because passive income sources are not stagnant. They grow over time. Rents on properties will go up. The stock market goes up over time. Your skills with your crafts increase.

You now have more than you need; much more. You've earned it with patience and discipline. It's a beautiful thing. No, it didn't happen overnight, but for those who didn't have a plan, they are no better off for having spent everything they made during those years you sacrificed. And you are here now.

Selfishly, I want this for you so you'll have even more time to dedicate to the other four aspects of the PEACE Legacy Formula. Legacy makers change the world. I'm very proud of you. I hope you'll dedicate even more time to being part of our cause and helping others make the journey you did.

At this level, you will also have new concerns to deal with, such as tax planning, multigenerational planning, and the creation of a foundation to support the causes you believe in. I hope you'll consider adding Abundance International to your list of charitable causes to support.

The Legacy Asset Plan

The Legacy Asset Plan is based on sound principles and financial literacy you'll find endorsed by many others. It may seem simplistic to you, and that's the beauty of it. Brilliance is not found in complexity, but in the effectiveness of the executed plan.

"It will take too long," some will say. Or "I don't want to wait that long to have what I want now."

You know the truth: good plans work for those who work them. But that's the real challenge. Not the plan. But most people won't do the very things they know would work. As a legacy maker, I know you're one of those who will get it done. And it's yours for the taking.

Financial Abundance for Generations

Estate and multigenerational asset planning brings new levels of complexity. But there are amazing people who specialize in crafting tailored strategies for

- Minimizing tax burdens
- Mitigating risk
- Directing assets for generations
- Achieving above-average return on investments
- Incorporating your personal values into your investment choices
- Increasing business entity valuations
- Creating succession and exit plans for your business
- Optimizing cash flow
- Securing quality medical care from anywhere in the world
- Increasing your expected healthy life expectancy

One of these advisors is P. J. DiNuzzo, who began his private wealth management firm in 1989 and currently manages close to one billion dollars in assets for his clients. He always begins his work by truly getting to know the hopes and dreams of his clients. But he also finds that many haven't really thought through what they want. Over the course of several introductory sessions, they work together to come up with a clearly defined set of goals, wishes, and plans for carrying on their legacy to the next generation.

Another private wealth manager is William Tate, who worked with the top New York and San Francisco investment firms before launching his own. He describes himself as the multigenerational wealth transfer and philanthropy mentor for mission-driven millionaires and their families. The way he works with clients is to ensure that their value systems are passed along to the next generation more than just their wealth.

At this level, it's nearly impossible to manage, or be the expert, in all the tasks and responsibilities of multigenerational wealth management. Management firms like these help by providing experts in each facet of your legacy, so you rest assured that who you are is part of your wealth management plan.

Business Funding Basics

Because one of the best ways to build substantial assets is through starting and growing a private business, I felt compelled to add a section in this Assets chapter on business funding. In many ways, I'm adding this section because it's one piece of content I wish I'd had years ago. I know that my lack of this knowledge with respect to business funding kept me from realizing some big dreams when I was in my thirties. Looking back, I can clearly see that if I'd known how to get my ideas into a presentable format, I had Mr. Rosati ready to present me to angel investors who would have gladly funded me upon his recommendation. We're talking about millions in funding at a time when the market and the idea were right.

I don't want that to happen to you. Rather, if you have a passion for a great idea, I'd like to help you clarify your idea, get it ready for presentation, and help you find the right venture capital partner who will help you pitch your idea to the right investor. When you're ready, go to Marcum-Davis.com/Legacy and look for the Legacy Business Funding program. I'd love to come alongside you with the right business packaging coaches to make these dreams come true if you'd like the help.

Briefly, here are the four principles for your Legacy Business Funding:

- Begin with the End in Mind
- Write Your Business Plan
- Create Your Pitch Deck
- Get in Front of the Right People

Begin with the End in Mind

You are the visionary. It's your passion that will sell the idea. But first, you need to be intimately familiar with what the world will look like when your idea has fully come to life. It starts with an idea that lights you up, but then you need to envision every aspect of the business.

- Who is your target customer?
- What are they buying now?
- How are you improving their current experience?
- How is your product created or software written?
- What vendors do you plan to hire who are a unique fit with your vision?
- How will you market and get the product vision in front of your target customer?
- How will you profitably deliver the product or service so that both of you want to repeat the experience?
- What do you personally love about your vision?

If you hire a business packaging consultant, they'll get into all of this with you, but you should have these basics under your belt for your own knowledge and preparedness.

The Business Plan

The actual business plan is a tool to help you clarify the steps needed to make your start-up work, or how your current business can get to the next level. It also demonstrates to investors that you know what you're talking about and that you've done your homework.

The US Small Business Administration has created a very good resource for outlining what would typically go into a business plan. They have a template for start-ups and existing businesses on their website that you can download.

Typically, investors like to see business plans that are around twenty-five pages long. Less may indicate you don't know enough, and more may come across as overselling. You'll have to find the right outline and length for your idea.

The Pitch Deck

The pitch deck is typically around ten pages in length. It's designed to sell your idea, show the potential, and convey why you believe there is a huge market opportunity for your vision. These are much more graphical and visually enticing, whereas business plans are typically all text. Think of it like a PowerPoint presentation. Get it down to a beautiful .pdf document so it can be shared.

Speaking of sharing your vision, you need to exercise extreme caution in who you give these documents to. In many cases, you'll want to get a nondisclosure and confidentiality agreement signed by the people receiving copies. The business world is filled with stories of ideas being stolen. However, if you have a chance to get an idea in front of an industry giant or top celebrity, you may have to send it on faith. A business packaging coach will guide you in these areas as well.

Getting in Front of the Right People

Now let's talk about finding the right investor for your vision. Part of your business planning will include your investment "ask"—the amount of investment money you're seeking. You've done the forecasting and budgeting to know how much you will need to get your dream to the levels you want. That ask could be anywhere from $500,000 or $50,000,000. You must justify why it's needed and how big it will get your business to grow and profit once you have it and have executed your plan. You may also suggest stages for funding over several months or a year. You'll also need to consider how much equity they are receiving for their investment, or whether you're looking for "debt financing," meaning a loan with repayment terms.

Once you have your ask numbers, that will help your business packaging coach to place you into different groups of potential investors who like doing those types of investments.

If you want to do this on your own, or perhaps you've already gone through this process in the past, you can certainly take your shot at it. You'll learn from each encounter and presentation. Keep in mind that it may require many presentations before you find the right investor.

Keep your passion high and envision your ideas as funded and living out their potential every morning when you wake up. You are the vision. You only lose when you lose your passion or quit trying.

Finally, know that Assets may be only one of the five aspects of the PEACE Legacy Formula, but it's one that can add peace and abundance to your life. Assets truly are the currency of your dreams.

If you need more resources and inspiration to help you build assets, visit MarcumDavis.com/Legacy.

Chapter 10:

Creations: Your Gifts Shared with the World

The meaning of life is to find your gift.
The purpose of life is to give it away.
—**PABLO PICASSO**

Beyond all other aspects of legacy building, creation is the most powerful. Why? Because it has the greatest opportunity to impact more people than you could ever touch personally.

Let me offer an example that you'll easily relate to. Tell me, what is your favorite music band or singer? Personally, I still love the music of AC/DC, Linkin Park, and Nickelback. Judge me now if you must, but I get such powerful energy from listening to their music. This music fuels my workouts and road trips.

But keep this in mind: I don't personally know any of these band members. They may be great people or jerks. I have no idea. In the case of Linkin Park, their lead singer, Chester Bennington, took his own life a number of years ago. Additionally, rockers are known for living lives of indulgence: "sex, drugs, and rock 'n' roll" as the saying goes. The stereotype isn't universal, however. Other musicians are known to be giving people and are associated with the causes they support. I still don't know them personally. But what I do know is that I have received positive emotions, inspiration, and motivation from their creations that have added to the quality of my life, even though they have no idea who I am or that what they created has benefited me personally.

This is the power of creation. Whether you build a skyscraper, write screenplays, create a business, start a nonprofit, paint murals, or record music, you can touch millions of people you may never meet. Although you may never meet them in person, your impact can go on long after you've left this world.

When Rick wrote his book, he had no idea a college professor would pick it up and ask him to speak at her class and how that would impact his future, or mine. But none of it would have happened if he hadn't disciplined himself to write the book in the first place.

The oil painting I use as the background for the book cover is from a Ukrainian artist named Anton Evmeshkin. I paid for the commercial rights to use the work, but he has no idea who I am or how much his use of paint on canvas added value to my life and this brand.

What can you create that can be shared with the world?

You Were Made to Create

It is said that we were made in the image of our Creator. The very first words of the Bible are "In the beginning God created . . ." Creating is part of our core essence. The highest level of Maslow's Hierarchy of Needs is "Self-Actualization." This is the expression of who we truly are. I believe that we must create to express what is within. If we don't, we feel stifled and unfulfilled. You have been given something to do and to create from the gifts placed within you from the beginning of time.

Conversely, going through life and not producing the creations you were given will be one of your greatest regrets.

Les Brown tells a parable that illustrates this better than anything I've heard:

> Imagine if you will, being on your deathbed and standing around your bed, the ghosts of the ideas, the dreams, the abilities, the talents given to you by life. And you, for whatever reason, you never acted on those ideas, you never pursued that dream, you never used your talents, we never saw your leadership, you never used your voice, you never wrote that book. And there they are standing around your bed looking at you with large angry eyes saying, "We came to you; and only you could have given us life. And now we must die with you forever." The question is, if you died today, what ideas, what dreams, what abilities, what talents, what gifts would die with you?

I remember Rick telling me, just two days before he died, "Marcum, God needs to give me another ten years. I've still got two books left in me." He didn't get that decade, but I take solace in knowing that the reason he wanted it so much was that he saw the immense good that came from writing the one book that touched so many people, became his purpose, changed his life, his daughter's life, and eventually mine.

I often look inside and ask myself whether there is more in me that needs to come out in a way that can benefit someone else. When my time comes, I don't want even one ghost standing by my bed of a dream given to me that I did not at least try to create and give it life. I want to create from my soul that which could be enjoyed and benefit others long after I'm gone. This book is one of those creations.

Most likely, you already know what has been given to you that needs to be created. It may be artistic, such as writing a book, creating a painting, making movies, or producing music. But it could also be a business or nonprofit endeavor that cries out for life from within you.

However, if you don't have an idea right now, and you feel stuck trying to figure out what has been given to you to create, make some quiet time to ask your spirit this deep and penetrating question: "What did the Creator imagine for me when he made me?" Ask with a deep emotional desire, from that quiet listening space, to actually want to know the answer to the question. Ask daily until answers begin to come. Just know that there is an answer to that question, and the Creator wants to bring it to life through you.

Creating Is Pure Joy

There is nothing as glorious as seeing something you've imagined be birthed and come to life. You'll be able to say, "Look! I did that!" This is why I love this subject so much. Creation of any kind is tangible proof of your time here. It's beautiful. And, best of all, the work to create it will be pure joy as well.

If you know Steven Spielberg's story as he tells it, as a young man he was so driven to make movies that he snuck onto the Universal Studio lot and found a trailer that wasn't being used and put his name on the door. He lived there and began networking to find a way to get started making movies. You can tell that every moment in the movie business has been pure joy for him.

It may not be that your creations are also your livelihood. It won't matter. Create anyway.

As I am writing this chapter in my favorite hookah café, the server asked me what I was doing. After telling her that I was writing a book, she told me her story. She had started writing a book to share her story of struggling to make life work as an immigrant and a young woman in her early twenties. But her family convinced her to stop; that it had no commercial value and she needed to focus on her education. She got married and never finished her education, or the book.

Now, quickly approaching forty, she waits tables and feels unfulfilled. But she has continued to write poetry for herself. Her soul needed to breathe her writings into life, no matter who would read it or whether it made money. Those outcomes are often realized after the work is done. As I encouraged her to just find twenty minutes each day to write and finish her book because someone out there needs to know they are not alone on their immigrant journey, she began to tear up. The idea touched her in a profound way. She's going to come back tomorrow and share some of her writings and poetry with me.

I know this tiny amount of encouragement was all she needed. I believe she'll get back to writing and finish the book she started. She needs to for the sake of her own soul so she can live with no regrets. I promise you, the moment she writes even one more sentence in her book, it will spark new life and joy from deep within her.

Don't Allow Excuses to Stop You

You may be familiar with the classic book *Think and Grow Rich* by Napoleon Hill. Although the book was written in 1937, it is still a bestseller and on the "must-read" lists of many business leaders today. What is less known is that he wrote a follow-up book the very next year titled *Outwitting the Devil*. It's a brilliant allegorical story of the devil revealing his schemes to a character named Mr. Earthbound, on how he keeps people trapped in busywork, and other devices, so they will never accomplish their purpose—their legacies. But it wasn't published until 2011—seventy-three years later and long after his death! Why?

Napoleon's wife, Annie Lou, convinced him that it was too controversial and could get them expelled from their church. The suggestion that a man would have a conversation with the devil, and that the devil would suggest that he even uses some church traditions to keep people from achieving, was too much for her. After his death, she passed the manuscript on to the Napoleon Hill Foundation with the condition that they would not publish it while she was alive. But the wife of the foundation president had the same concerns and asked that it not be published until after her passing as well. Finally, it became available to the world in 2011 and stands as another masterpiece of insights and wisdom that was denied to two generations of people. Read it. You'll be amazed, and yet saddened, that so many people never had the opportunity to read it because of the fears of "concerned" family members.

Like Napoleon Hill, and the waitress I mentioned earlier, you may have well-intentioned friends and family members tell you that your ideas have no value. They may not see it as you see it. *But it wasn't given to them to create.* Listening to them, instead of the voice within you, may lead to a regret you'll carry all your life. I'm not suggesting that you don't get feedback from supportive people, and even a few nonattached critics, but they shouldn't be given veto power over your calling.

The number of excuses people have for not giving life to their gifts is long, and most of them are very real. I don't question that. If creating was easy, it wouldn't have the same value. But for every excuse, there is an answer. Do you think you need money first? Do you think you're too old or too young? Do you think you just don't have the network of people and resources necessary to make it happen? For every excuse, there are thousands of stories of people who had the same excuse, and more, who kept moving forward with determination until it happened.

During my time in Silicon Valley, I learned one thing about venture capitalists. They fund great ideas and people with passion. Anyone can hire top talent and people with technical skills, and anyone can pay for marketing. It's the idea that has value to the marketplace. Funding follows great ideas and passionate people. Period.

What's your excuse? Perhaps you've been seduced by busyness and don't think you have the time. Maybe laziness clouds your ambitions like a wet blanket. You have to fight your way out of your excuses. If nothing else, be motivated by this: regret is heavier than all efforts to at least try. It's the heaviest of all burdens. Don't let it happen to you. Fight for your dreams and create what you were given to create. The world will be better for it, and we'll all thank you.

Don't Keep Your Creations in a Closet

Can you imagine Leonardo da Vinci painting the *Mona Lisa*, and then leaving it in a closet so no one saw it? Yet we see examples of this all around us. I was even guilty of this at one time. In the '00s, I recorded music in my home studio. It was a combination of instrumental pieces and songs with lyrics. It was a pure joy and expression from my soul when I recorded them, but they languished on a computer hard drive for nearly a decade until I published them on my website (You can listen to them at MarcumDavis.com/Legacy.). It was encouraging to get feedback from others on how the music touched them. My music may never reach any charts, but I finished the process of making them available. How they will impact people is up to God, but they're available now.

In truth, I hadn't really thought about sharing them. It felt like a private and personal expression for myself. I've found so many other people who feel the same way about their art. Many of us feel shy about sharing what we've made. The fear of criticism can be overwhelming, but the gifts inside of us were given for a reason. Imagine if King David kept his poems, the Psalms, to himself because he felt they were just private journals.

In reality, we are responsible for more than just the creation of our gifts; we are also responsible for finding ways to share them.

We are blessed beyond comprehension to be alive today. It was only a few decades ago that the world became available to us through the internet. You can now reach the entire planet with just a YouTube video. The gifts within you, and your unique message to the world, can reach billions of people in a way that was unimaginable in the '70s. Best of all, most of it is free and available to you right now.

However, decades later, it seems that everyone is online and the volume of noise can drown out the attention you need to give your creation. You're going to need a strategy for allowing the world to be exposed to the art that is within you.

Look at others who have created similar works and see how they shared their art. They may look uber successful now, but see if you can uncover their humble beginnings. All artists had to start somewhere. Success leaves clues and patterns you can replicate to get your craft to the world. You'll need to do the work, but it's worth it.

- Take a class on online marketing
- Get others who have an audience to share your work
- Start a podcast and YouTube channel to gain subscribers
- Hire marketers with specific expertise in your niche
- Attend events where you can display your work

Internet marketer John Reese has said that the money is not in your email list but in other people's email lists. Get others to share your craft with their audiences. Whether money or awareness is your goal, the fastest way to gain exposure is to have *others* talk about it and share it with their lists, and for you to be a guest on their platforms.

Follow patterns for success and don't let your creations be a *Mona Lisa* that never gets out of the closet.

Turning Your Creations into a Business

A wonderful friend of mine is Dale Mathis, a sculptor of creative decor that defies imagination. I first saw his work at a gallery in South Lake Tahoe, California, nearly twenty years ago. The works were breathtaking, unusual, and inspiring. He incorporates moving gears and light into wall pieces, desks, and other unique showpieces. He's now cultivated an international following and clients from among the elite achievers of the world.

However, when he started, he made a critical mistake many artists make: he fell in love with his own work. Now that may sound counter-intuitive, so allow me to explain. There were some styles of work that he personally loved, but which weren't selling. And the ones that seemed to be selling felt less impressive by his tastes. At first, he hated the idea of just selling his lesser works because that's what people were buying. "I don't want to just make wall clocks!" he bemoaned. But he realized that if he wanted to make a living from his craft, he'd have to love his work as a business even more than be in love with particular pieces in his collection.

"I quickly realized that I couldn't buy enough of my own works to make a living. I had to decide to listen to what the customers were wanting and give it to them," he lamented. "But, in doing so, I've found ways to evolve my work to give people what they love and expect from me, mix it with elements of my art that I loved most, and make a great living from it. I had to remove my ego and become as good a businessman as I was an artist." Give yourself the treat of seeing what he does at DaleMathis.com.

The business of art must be treated as a business. Many creative types refuse to listen to what consumers are telling them and end up as starving artists. Yes, business skills are very different from artistic skills, and many creators resist the obvious need to hone their business skills.

You'll need to learn more about promoting, marketing, mass production, contracts, and cash management. These skills seem foreign to creative personalities, but they will make the difference between making a career from your craft or remaining a starving artist.

There are no shortcuts to success. No cutting corners. But your love and passion for your creations should drive you to do whatever it takes to share your magic with the world and make a good living while doing it.

Create! We can't wait to see the beautiful expressions from your soul.

If you need more resources and inspiration to help you create, visit MarcumDavis.com/Legacy.

Chapter 11:

Expressions of Kindness: A Lifestyle of Service

We can make a difference and make the world
a better place by expressing kindness and compassion
to ourselves, to others, and to the planet.
—DEEPAK CHOPRA

E xpressions of kindness to others is one of the most personally fulfilling aspects of the PEACE Legacy Formula.

A life of service is something that speaks to our souls. It's not
about material wealth or personal accomplishments. It's about making a
positive impact on the world and the people around us. It gives us a sense
of purpose, fulfillment, and satisfaction that can't be found anywhere else.
And I'll tell you this, it's not just the people being helped that benefit; it's
the person serving too. It's an opportunity for personal growth and development, and that comforting sense that you added value to someone.

One of the biggest benefits of your expressions of kindness is the sense of purpose it provides. When you dedicate your time and energy to helping others, you often find that you receive far more in return than you give. That feeling of fulfillment and happiness is a direct result of making a difference in someone else's life. It gives you a reason to get up in the morning and makes your life feel more meaningful and valuable.

Often overlooked is the beautiful opportunity for personal growth and development. When we give in service to others, we learn new skills, gain insights, and develop a deeper understanding of why you are here. These experiences broaden our horizons and help us grow in ways that we never knew possible.

And let's not forget about the impact that kindness has on the people and communities being helped. Even small acts of kindness can make a big difference in someone's life, and that impact can have a ripple effect that extends far beyond the initial act of service. That's what makes a life of service so meaningful. It gives individuals the opportunity to make a lasting difference in the world.

Even more, expressions of kindness bring people together and foster a sense of community. When we work together to help others, we build relationships and create bonds that last a lifetime. Those connections and the memories that come with them become an important part of a person's legacy. They're remembered and cherished by those who were touched by their kindness. Have you worked on a project in a way that you felt a connection with everyone involved? When you see those team members, do you still talk about those days?

So, my friend, when you dedicate yourself to expressions of kindness as part of who you are in this world, you'll find that it leads to a meaningful and fulfilling life, and one that leaves a positive impact on the world. Isn't that what it's all about?

In the decade from 2011 to 2021, I hosted a weekly live stream that was a mix of relationship advice and personal development training. I hosted several mastermind groups and events. Thousands of people connected and more than five million viewed the videos on YouTube.

But what meant the most to me were the emails, letters, and messages of gratitude and encouragement that came in almost daily. One of my favorites was a handwritten letter I received in the mail with a $50 bill enclosed. The letter was from a man in Phoenix who shared with me that he and his wife had started listening to my broadcasts and how it rejuvenated their twenty-two-year marriage with new life and passion. The $50 was for me to buy a few cigars for myself since he'd heard I enjoyed them from time to time.

It's truly amazing and humbling to hear from people you've never met who say that you made a positive impact on their lives. Seriously amazing.

I've always felt that my role was to share what has been given to me and trust that God will get it to whoever needs it. No matter whether a video had ten views or fifty thousand, it just meant that those are the ones who needed to see it.

Bruce Wilkinson wrote a little thought book called *The Prayer of Jabez*. He expounded a verse in the Bible with his modern-day interpretations. It went on to sell nine million copies. The verse was 1 Chronicles 4:10, "He was the one who prayed to the God of Israel, 'Oh, that you would bless me and expand my territory! Please be with me in all that I do and keep me from all trouble and pain!' And God granted him his request."

Anytime something says, "And God granted his request," we should stop and pay attention to what was being asked! Bruce expanded on this idea of "expanding our territory" to include anyone we may come in contact with as part of our territory. He teaches that we should keep our awareness on alert with the understanding that the people we encounter may have been placed in our path for a reason so we could offer something of value, as I did with the waitress I mentioned earlier. It may be that the person standing in line with you at Starbucks just suffered a major setback, and your encouragement could change their entire focus. It may be that another person has the exact resource you need for accomplishing a purpose you are passionate about that God sent your way. Expand your awareness of the ways you can add value to people around you, and how they may add value to you as well. But nothing happens without this awareness and taking the action to say something in the moment.

When I think about expressions of kindness, I find that they may come in several forms:

1. Words of encouragement

2. Offers of material help

3. Charitable endeavors

I know this section is close to your heart, so let's go a little deeper into these three categories now.

Words of Encouragement

One word, one sentence, or one gesture of support can transform someone's life forever.

Think about it. How many times in your life have you been struggling with a challenge, feeling discouraged, and then someone came along and gave you the push you needed to keep going? That person believed in you, and their belief gave you the strength and motivation to achieve your goals.

Now, I challenge you to be that person for someone else. Here are three ways you can offer encouragement to those around you:

1. Acknowledge their strengths: We all have unique talents and abilities, but sometimes we forget just how talented we truly are. Take the time to acknowledge someone's strengths and let them know how much you admire their abilities. This will help them recognize their own value and potential.

2. Help them find solutions: When someone is facing a challenge, they may feel overwhelmed and unsure of how to proceed. By offering support and brainstorming solutions with them, you can

help them gain clarity and confidence. This will enable them to take action and move forward with purpose.

3. Celebrate their wins: When someone achieves a goal, no matter how small, it's important to celebrate their success. By recognizing and celebrating their accomplishments, you are showing them that their hard work and effort are valued and appreciated. This will motivate them to continue striving for excellence. It actually programs their nervous system to want to do more.

Become a champion of encouragement. By offering support and motivation to those around you, you are helping to create a world where everyone can achieve their dreams. Let's work together to uplift and inspire one another to greatness.

Offers of Material Help

There is a transformative power of helping others in their time of financial need. When someone is struggling to make ends meet, a kind and generous gesture can have a tremendous impact on their life, lifting them up to the next level and out of a tough spot.

However, it's important to approach these situations with caution. It's crucial to know when to give financially and when not to. Sometimes, giving money can enable bad habits or poor financial decisions, leading to more problems down the line. But there are also times when giving money can make a positive and life-changing difference.

Here are three examples of good times to help someone in financial need:

1. Emergencies: When someone is facing an unexpected financial emergency, such as a medical emergency or a sudden job loss, it can be difficult for them to stay afloat. In these cases, offering financial support can be life-saving.

2. Education: Education is one of the most powerful tools we have for lifting ourselves out of poverty. If someone you know is strug-

gling to afford their education, offering financial support can enable them to pursue their dreams and build a better future.

3. Entrepreneurship: Starting a business can be a game changer for someone who is struggling financially. However, it often requires an initial investment. If you believe in someone's business idea and see potential for success, offering financial support can be a wise investment in their future.

Helping someone in need when they can do nothing in return for you is one of the most rewarding and satisfying experiences you can have. It allows you to make a difference in someone's life, and the positive impact can ripple outward to their family and community.

Yes, we want to approach helping others in their time of financial need with caution and discernment. But let us also be open to the possibility that making a life-changing difference in someone's life may be the right thing to do at the right time.

Receiving Changes Lives Too

Some move too far to one side of giving, in that they become bad at receiving. A friend of mine named Jim was one of these people. He loved giving but never wanted to receive anything. He didn't want to owe anyone anything and felt that receiving created an unspoken obligation. In fact, he actually became somewhat obnoxious in his refusal to accept gifts until I told him this truth: he was training others not to be giving people.

Imagine if you were the one who loved your friendship with Jim and took the time to really think about something you thought he'd love, only to have him fight with you and refuse to accept it! It would ruin your day and possibly create some bad feelings with him.

What's worse, you'd become less likely to want to give in the future. That's right. If we receive gifts badly, it actually trains people to be less giving in other areas of their life because they had such a bad experience with us.

Imagine, on the other hand, if you were to receive a gift warmly and with joy, thanking the person for such kindness. You would make them feel wonderful for having taken the time to find the gift and give it. You would literally be programming their nervous system that there are wonderful rewards for giving. You truly train every person you warmly receive a gift from to become a bigger giver in every part of their life, and many others will be blessed by them because you were a good receiver.

Receiving has little to do with the gift, whether you actually want, like, or need it. It has to do with creating more givers in this world. I hope that hits home with you and that you'll make sure you're creating more giving people on this planet by making everyone who gives anything to you very glad they did.

Charitable Endeavors

If there is one thing I'm most proud of in my legacy, it's my dedication to the work we've done to bring aid to the orphans in Ukraine. One hundred percent of all royalties from this book will go to Abundance International to continue their mission to help these children who don't deserve the hardships placed on them by war.

I loved the eight years leading up to the war when we spent time with the kids on our visits. More than the construction projects or deliveries of food and supplies, it was pure joy to be able to play with them and see their smiles. Often, they would make crafts for us, sing a song, or put on a little pageant. I would never have guessed what was ahead for us when the Russians invaded, but I'm glad we were there to do as much good as we could.

You don't need to be on foreign soil in order to find ways to give. There are many ways to help those in need who can do nothing in return. Needs are all around you. Listen to your heart and respond.

This is one of the most important and satisfying things you will do.

Giving is not just about writing a check or making a donation. It's about having a giving heart, overflowing with compassion, and having a desire to make a positive impact on the world.

When we give from a place of love and generosity, we can create profound change and transform the lives of those less fortunate. Here are five ways you can give to help those in need, support causes you believe in, or start a charity or foundation for something you believe in:

1. Donate your time: Giving your time to help others is one of the most meaningful ways to give. You can volunteer at a local shelter, church, food bank, or hospital. You can also mentor someone who is struggling or simply be a listening ear for someone who needs it.

2. Make a financial donation: Giving money to a charity or organization that aligns with your values and beliefs is a powerful way to make a difference. Whether it's a one-time donation or a recurring contribution, every dollar counts.

3. Give your expertise: If you have a particular skill or area of expertise, consider giving your time and knowledge to a cause or organization that could benefit from it. For example, you could offer pro bono consulting services to a nonprofit or teach a class on financial literacy for a community organization.

4. Start a charity or foundation: If there is a cause or issue that you are particularly passionate about, consider starting a charity or foundation to support it. This can be a powerful way to create long-term change and make a meaningful impact on the world.

5. Support small businesses: When you buy from small businesses or local artisans, you are not only supporting their livelihood, but you are also contributing to the economic growth of your community.

Giving is not just about the act of giving. It's about cultivating a giving heart and mindset, where compassion and generosity overflow from within. By finding ways to give our time, money, expertise, and support to those in need, we can create a world where everyone has the opportunity to thrive and succeed.

If you need more resources and inspiration to help you incorporate expressions of kindness into your daily living, visit MarcumDavis.com/Legacy.

PART 4

PART 4:

Why You Should Become a Legacy Maker

I f you've come this far, you have everything you need to become a legacy maker. All you need to do is take action—simple action following the PEACE Legacy Formula—every day.

Before we get into the last three chapters of this book, let me ask you some questions.

What would life be like if you developed deep, meaningful relationships with growth-minded people who loved and supported you deeply?

And what would it be like if you organized your days around building intentional, enjoyable experiences, instead of the "typical" way people live, overscheduling themselves with activities they don't really enjoy and obligations to other people's agendas?

How would you feel if ten years from now, you took inventory of your life and found countless creations that would ensure your beliefs, talents, and message for the world would be preserved long into the future?

And what if you also found assets that could support you in your later years while safeguarding important possessions and money for loved ones? Or if you knew that the assets you accumulated had been structured to support causes that were important to you even after your death?

And finally, what if you spent your days surrounded by kindness, from you, and to you?

It's not hard to conclude that life would feel pretty good if that were your life, don't you think?

Becoming a legacy maker is, by definition, the most personally fulfilling thing you can do. It builds a life you love and helps you pass on a legacy of your choosing to the next generation—and, many times, for generations to come.

And, ultimately, your legacy is the bridge to what I call the "Eternal You." In so many ways, our legacies help us live on through our relationships, experiences, creations, assets, and expressions of kindness that create ripples of kindness throughout the world. But our legacies are much more than a collection of things people say about us or that we pass along to the world. They are the bridge between our earthly lives and our spiritual beings.

To paraphrase Pierre Teilhard de Chardin, whom I quote in chapter 14, we are all spiritual beings having human experiences. When our human experience ends and our spiritual journey continues, the only thing that will touch on both sides of our lives is the legacy we each built.

That's what I'm going to talk about in this final part of the book.

First, I'm going to share how becoming a legacy maker is the most personally fulfilling thing you can do.

Then I'm going to share real-world examples showing how simple it is to live your life as a legacy maker in a way that passes along whatever is important to you to the next generation.

And, finally, I'm going to discuss the "Eternal You" and how to use your life of PEACE to build yourself a bridge to your true spiritual identity.

Because, when all is said and done, your legacy isn't just about what will be left of you when your human experience ends. It's about what will live on.

Your legacy is about building the most fulfilling life in the present while simultaneously passing along what's important to you to the next generation and creating a bridge between who you are today and what comes next after your earthly time comes to an end.

All you need to do is get started.

Chapter 12:

Because It's the Most Personally Fulfilling Thing You Can Do

Don't ask yourself what the world needs.
Ask yourself what makes you come alive, and go do that,
because what the world needs is people who have come alive.
—HOWARD THURMAN

What if the key to happiness is found not in the attainment of certain goals but in the pursuit of worthwhile goals instead?

That's a question many authors, philosophers, and researchers have addressed either directly or indirectly throughout the years. And it's one I have personally spent time asking myself as I have continued my personal pursuit of legacy making and helped thousands of other people achieve theirs.

And the more I consider that question, the more I realize that true happiness doesn't ever seem to be found once you reach a certain destination, although those are beautiful moments. It comes from identifying a destination of deep importance and then pursuing it in such a way that fulfills you while pursuing it so you don't only enjoy the outcome but the process as well.

In other words, personal fulfillment doesn't come as much from achieving a goal. It comes from pursuing that goal in a meaningful, enjoyable, and rewarding way.

And that's exactly what the PEACE Legacy Formula is designed to do. It's designed to help you *feel* the peace of pursuing something meaningful—your legacy—from the moment you make the commitment to do so. It helps you *feel* your legacy even before you've built it.

How?

Imagine for a moment that you are pursuing something that's values-driven, like we talked about in chapter 2. You want to set up your family for generations to come and leave a meaningful mark on your community and the world around you. Perhaps it involves something like me with Abundance International, through which I created a structure and support system to help Ukrainian orphans in a way that can continue long after my time on earth is over.

Although I founded and grew Abundance International before I identified the PEACE Legacy Formula, each element of the formula is now obvious in how I built it as I look back at what makes the organization effective and sustainable.

To begin, I built several relationships with people who share my deep desire to help Ukrainian orphans. Some of those people help raise funds, source materials, and maintain the safety and security for those incredible Ukrainian children. I also built many relationships with people who invest time, money, or both to ensure the resources we need are secured and delivered in a way that helps the orphans.

I also built experiences that support the orphans to ensure the children are not just provided with their basic needs but that they also feel the joy of meaningful experiences from people who love and care for them. I even incorporate experiences into some of my efforts to raise additional funds and support for the organization, such as by displaying pictures and videos of how we support those children on our website and in news appearances so other people can share a piece of the experience of supporting children with me. I also developed experiences to help raise support for those children to strengthen and continue operations beyond what I could possibly do alone.

As you might imagine, I built, managed, and invested substantial assets to support the organization and its operations so we could help even more orphans and create additional revenue streams to continue to grow and enjoy even more stability and peace of mind from a financial perspective.

I created content to support our operations, structures to strengthen our operations, and systems to be able to scale our operations, including, for example, this book. Every penny of royalties earned from my publisher for this book goes directly to Abundance International to support those children.

Moreover, the very foundation of Abundance International is to create and facilitate expressions of kindness, to the children first and foremost, along with our support team, our financial supporters, and others.

Imagine for a moment that this was your daily life. This is what you do all day. This is how you live.

How quickly would you begin to feel personal fulfillment? One day? One week? One year? Would you need to wait until you helped one hundred orphans before you felt joy and fulfillment? One thousand?

The truth is, you would begin to feel the warmth, joy, and PEACE the moment your journey began. When you're pursuing something so meaningful to you—whether for orphans in Ukraine, yourself, your family members, or your community around you—the PEACE Legacy Formula almost forces you to live your life in a way that's tremendously personally fulfilling.

By definition, you build relationships with people with whom you share common interests.

By definition, you develop experiences you enjoy that you *know* will lead to a result you desire greatly.

By definition, you build assets to support and further the cause you so deeply desire to pursue.

By definition, you create many things that will help you reach more people and scale much bigger than you possibly could if you had to do everything yourself. And you would create things that will last far beyond the years you have left to live on this planet.

By definition, you will create countless expressions of kindness both through your work and through your pursuit of your purpose—an act that independently leads to tremendous joy and many acts of kindness in return. As the old saying goes, "Kindness is contagious."

By definition, you bring PEACE to the world and PEACE to yourself when you follow the Legacy Formula while pursuing something so important to you.

And that's what a joyful and personally fulfilling day-to-day life looks like.

In the present.

By committing to and then taking action toward building your very own personal legacy, you truly can begin to defeat the dissatisfaction that way too many people experience every day.

Defeating Dissatisfaction

Unfortunately, dissatisfaction with life seems to be rampant in the world today. Many people feel stuck in jobs and trapped by obligations. There are few emotional states as crushing as the feeling of being trapped and unfulfilled. Sadly, what Henry David Thoreau said in 1854 appears to still ring true today, that "The mass of men live lives of quiet desperation."

When researching for this book, I was disheartened to discover that identifying an example of this principle was not very challenging. For example, Freddie Mercury, the late singer of the British rock band Queen, once confessed that, "You can have everything in the world and still be the loneliest man. And that is the most bitter type of loneliness. Success has brought me world idolization and millions of pounds. But it's prevented me from having the one thing we all need: A loving, ongoing relationship."

In 2010, actress Anne Hathaway was interviewed by actress, filmmaker, and humanitarian Angelina Jolie for an interview that was published in *Interview* magazine. The interview covered a number of topics, from Hathaway's defining moments to romantic relationships.

In the middle of the interview, Jolie asked Hathaway, in what seemed like an almost "throwaway" question, "So, what do you fear in life?"

By this point in her career, Hathaway had already appeared in several blockbuster projects, including *Get Smart, Bride Wars, The Princess Diaries,* and *The Devil Wears Prada,* to name just a few. She could have likely opened any door in the US or even worldwide with just a mention of her name. There was likely very little she could want but not have in the world given her financial prowess, name recognition, and network.

So what was her biggest fear?

Loneliness.

"Loneliness is my least favorite thing about life. The thing that I'm most worried about is just being alone without anybody to care for or someone who will care for me. That horrible feeling of isolation is something that I hope I never have to deal with again."[4]

How could this happen? How could rich and famous people, the ideal lifestyle to so many of us, find themselves in an emotional wasteland that brings them to wishing to end their lives or fearing that they might be alone without anyone to care for or someone who will care for them?

Not talking specifically about any of these particular individuals, because I don't know them personally, but you don't have to look hard to find stories of addiction, self-harm, anxiety, and depression in celebrities.

---

4   "Anne Hathaway," interview by Angelina Jolie, *Interview,* July 27, 2010, https://www.interviewmagazine.com/film/anne-hathaway.

But why? Is it the wealth, the fame, or both that causes so much dissatisfaction? Although there doesn't seem to be a bright-line rule that applies to everyone, it seems as though it is more common for *fame* to generally have a greater negative impact than *wealth* does, which makes sense to me. As the actor Bill Murray famously noted, "I always want to say to people who want to be rich and famous: 'try being rich first.' See if that doesn't cover most of it. There's not much downside to being rich, other than paying taxes and having your relatives ask you for money. But when you become famous, you end up with a 24-hour job."

There seems to be a lot we can learn from the impact of fame and fortune on celebrities and well-known businesspeople. Reflecting back to the PEACE Legacy Formula, it's easy to see how fame naturally impacts at least a couple of the Legacy Formula elements in a negative way.

For example, a 2009 study published in the *Journal of Phenomenological Psychology* found, among other things, that celebrity negatively impacts several areas that impact the Legacy Formula, including loss of privacy, family impact concerns, mistrust, and isolation.[5]

Moreover, in a 2019 piece published in *Insider*,[6] psychologist Sarah Davies indicated that the roles actors and performers play "become an increasing part of an identity" and when those roles end, especially roles they played for a long time, "there can be a process of loss and of grieving that part." Many actors echoed this in the piece, with *Game of Thrones* actor Kit Harington indicating that "taking off [his character] Jon Snow's costume felt like he was being 'skinned.'"

The more I learn about legacy building and personal fulfillment, the more I understand why celebrities across all genres so frequently feel dissatisfied or disconnected: so much of their existence involves getting into

5   Donna Rockwell and David C. Giles, "Being a Celebrity: A Phenomenology of Fame," *Journal of Phenomenological Psychology* 40, no. 2 (October 1, 2009): 178–210, https://doi.org/10.1163/004726609x12482630041889.

6   Lindsay Dodgson, "Stars like Kit Harington Often Seek Help after Losing an Iconic Character Role. We Asked Actors and Mental Health Experts Why." *Insider*, August 29, 2019, https://www.insider.com/mental-health-of-actors-suffers-when-long-series-ends-rehab-2019-8.

character, either on stage or behind a camera, and performing in a way that others expect or demand of them, irrespective of what they desire. Even professional athletes deal with this, so frequently being told to just "shut up and play."

With so much pressure to be what other people want them to be, it's no surprise to me that many rich and famous people struggle with dissatisfaction.

Improving Personal Satisfaction with a Growth Mindset

Tom Bilyeu, entrepreneur and cofounder of Quest Nutrition, which he built and sold for more than one billion dollars, and Impact Theory, a new media company, talks frequently about how to empower people to achieve their full potential. Among other things, Bilyeu's hypothesis is that a combination of your mindset, continuing personal growth, and the discovery of your life's purpose will lead to personal fulfillment.

With respect to mindset, for example, Bilyeu compares the difference between adopting a growth mindset versus a fixed mindset. A growth mindset is adopting the viewpoint that intelligence and abilities can be constantly improved through hard work and dedication and that there are almost no limits on human potential. On the other hand, someone with a fixed mindset believes there's a limit to how intelligent or skilled someone can become, no matter how hard they try.

Which one is right? Is there truly no limit to how intelligent, capable, or successful we can become? Can we defy the laws of physics? Or do we all have natural limits? In my research, the answer is that, with rare exception, growth-minded people will accomplish vastly more than those who limit what they believe they can do from the onset. Sure, I might never be able to slam dunk a basketball against a star NBA player. But with consistent work and practice, I can become better and better and better at whatever I'm passionate about.

The Legacy Formula is designed to check each of these boxes, and more.

Being growth minded touches every element in the Legacy Formula. For example, fixed-minded people might believe the potential for their marriage, relationships, or friendships is low. Growth-minded people know they truly *can* have deep, loving relationships if they continue to work on improving them. Moreover, fixed-minded people might believe there are only so many assets they will be able to accumulate because of their current job or financial situation. Growth-minded people know that their current financial situation only reflects what they've done in the past, and their ability to build assets in the future will depend on the actions they take in the present and moving forward.

Consistently generating creations you're passionate about makes your days much more enjoyable. You wake up every morning loving everything about your day, looking forward to all the opportunities to work on your passions at work and at play. You love your job and the impact your work has on the world. You spend personal time pursuing hobbies you've enjoyed your whole life. You love your life.

And surrounding yourself with people you love and then creating memorable experiences and expressions of kindness cultivates deep relationships.

The Legacy Formula is designed to put you in a position to love your life, not just for what you're building for the future, but also in the present moment.

Your Joy Booster

When you commit to becoming a legacy maker, you're essentially committing to setting and pursuing a series of small but important goals that lead you to a large and even more important goal.

The small goals are simple and follow the exact PEACE Legacy Formula:

- People and Close Relationships
- Experiences Shared
- Assets Left to Heirs

- Creations Enjoyed by Many
- Expressions of Kindness

And the big goal, of course, is to leave a legacy of your own choosing so your family, friends, and community will continue to be impacted long after you pass away.

Why is this important?

Because science tells us that achieving goals releases dopamine that gives us a physical and emotional sense of accomplishment, fulfillment, and satisfaction. For example, in an article posted on *Psychology Today*, Ralph Ryback MD wrote that "when we get something we want—a promotion, an ice cream cone, or a kiss from a loved one—our brain releases dopamine. This chemical is often known as the 'feel-good' neurotransmitter because it does just that—it makes us feel good."[7] But he took this effect one step further, suggesting, "It's possible to manipulate your dopamine levels by setting small goals and then accomplishing them. For instance, your brain may receive a spike in dopamine if you promise yourself that you'll clean out the refrigerator, and then you do."

In other words, consistently setting and achieving meaningful goals releases your body's natural "feel good" medicine, dopamine, giving you a sense of accomplishment, fulfillment, and satisfaction. It's an overall state of being I describe as joy.

Here's how it works:

1. Setting a goal: When we set a goal, whether it's to complete a task or achieve a long-term objective, our brain releases dopamine in anticipation of the reward we will receive once we accomplish the goal.

2. Working toward the goal: As we work toward the goal, our brain continues to release dopamine in response to our progress and

---

7   Ralph Ryback, MD, "The Science of Accomplishing Your Goals," *Psychology Today*, October 3, 2016, https://www.psychologytoday.com/ie/blog/the-truisms-wellness/201610/the-science-accomplishing-your-goals.

achievements. This gives us a sense of accomplishment and motivation to keep going.

3. Achieving the goal: Once we achieve the goal, our brain releases a surge of dopamine, which gives us a sense of fulfillment and satisfaction. This reinforces the behavior that led to the accomplishment and encourages us to set new goals and continue striving for success.

In addition to goal achievement, dopamine is also released in response to pleasurable experiences such as food, sex, and social interactions. This reinforces these behaviors and encourages us to seek out similar experiences in the future. Thus, your work on developing deep relationships during your journey toward building your legacy will naturally release dopamine on a regular basis.

My point is simply that science, and your own biology, will support you and add joy to your life while doing the very things you want most for your legacy. This isn't just a program to create your last will and testament to leave for heirs after you're gone. A legacy maker's life is filled with more joy *today*, and every day, as we move toward our goals.

Experiencing Inner Joy Even in Crisis

As I discussed briefly in chapter 6, by the time the bombs started landing in Ukraine, friends and family had been encouraging me to escape for months. And those pleas only grew louder when the bombing began. They grew even louder when some of my worst fears came true in April 2022, when a bomb landed right in the playground of one the largest orphanages Abundance International supports, shattering windows and damaging the property but, thankfully, not harming any of the children, who had been evacuated before the bombs hit.

Even as I assessed the damage, however, I knew that I still could not leave Ukraine. The orphanages had only partially adjusted to the new reality, and there were other orphanages in need of our support. I wouldn't travel out of Ukraine until I knew the orphanages had everything they needed to serve and protect the children and a network set in place to continue the support.

Why do I share that story in the context of joy? Because during those moments, stepping over shards of broken glass and assessing the aftermath of a bomb landing where the children used to regularly kick soccer balls to each other, the most powerful emotion that occupied my body was not fear but gratitude. I didn't feel demoralized; I felt motivated. I didn't feel hate; I felt love. I felt tremendous personal fulfillment for being called to serve those children to the best of my ability. I felt a tremendous sense of peace in my heart, even as my eyes scanned the aftermath of war. I was exactly where I was supposed to be.

How is that possible? Had I been simply "based" in Ukraine because I liked the country without ties to serve others or connection to causes greater than myself, I'm *sure* I would have left before Russia invaded or, at the very latest, as soon as possible after the invasion began. But I was there not just for myself but to serve thousands of children who needed me. My work there wasn't yet complete. And the surge of power and energy I felt with every act I took to help improve conditions for those children outweighed any fleeting moments of fear or anxiety I experienced.

Of course, you don't need to find yourself in the middle of a war zone to get the personal fulfillment you can experience from serving others. Even random acts of kindness, feeding a parking meter for someone whose meter is about to expire, or paying for the person behind you in line at the coffee shop, can release small rushes of dopamine, the positive reward molecule, to make you glad you did it.

The point is, intentionally working through the PEACE Legacy Formula on a daily basis sets you up not just for successfully building a legacy that's important to you, but it also sets you up to experience tremendous joy and fulfillment along the way.

How Service to Others Creates Dopamine Rewards

What if there was a formula for happiness that you could activate at any given moment in time? What would that look like? For the sake of simplicity, let's presume that happiness is a state of positive emotions and a sense of satisfaction. That seems to be a universal definition. So, what creates positive and negative emotions?

Negative emotions can be boiled down to two categories: pain and the fear of impending pain. Although this life will include true suffering, such as a health challenge, financial loss, or lost relationship, most of our negative emotional experiences come from our imagination, our fear of sufferings that haven't happened yet, and may never happen. I call such fears a misuse of our imagination. Fear is not why we were given the ability to imagine. As the Scripture says, "Perfect love casts out all fear." (1 John 4:18, New International Version) I'd estimate that as much as 95 percent of all of our negative emotions are related to this second category and are completely unnecessary.

Positive emotions similarly come from two primary categories: accomplishment and reward. Accomplishments are the basis for most of our goals. We see a point in the future where, if we reach it, we will have hit a milestone where we can declare that we won. It may be a degree, a raise, the purchase of our dream house or car, or retirement. But it culminates in a moment in time when we feel positive emotions for that accomplishment. But how long does that last? A day? A week? A month? After the emotional peak, there also comes an emotional low when the joy of the accomplishment wanes and we ask ourselves, "Now what?"

The lasting state of positive emotion comes from reward, but not in the same way as accomplishment. This reward is built into our biology to recognize and reward us for movement in the direction of meaningful activity. These emotions are triggered by the chemical dopamine, also known as the "happiness molecule." Dopamine is triggered by many activities we engage in, such as exercise, sex, and play. But its purpose is to reward us for taking steps in a direction that will serve us best. It's God's way of keeping us happy about moving forward in the direction of good behaviors. But the most important way we can utilize this reward system is to intentionally engage in services that will add to our legacy.

So how does this all work? Simply put, service to others can create dopamine rewards by activating the brain's reward system through social connections, progress, and positive feedback.

For example, when we help others, we activate the brain's reward system through feelings of empathy and altruism. This can lead to the release of dopamine, which creates a sense of pleasure and reward.

Moreover, we often receive positive feedback as a result of serving others, such as gratitude or appreciation. We also tend to build social connections and relationships with generous, positive, others-driven people. We connect with others with whom we have much in common, such as a generous heart and compassion for common causes. And we also tend to develop a sense of purpose to our lives much bigger than ourselves.

Imagine for a moment that you spend a good bit of your time living *that* reality, serving others, building relationships with generous people with whom you share common interests and passions, being thanked and appreciated for time and money spent serving others, and living a life of purpose much greater than you. It doesn't take a big leap of logic to understand how personally fulfilling that existence will be.

In every way you can imagine, being a legacy maker can be the most personally fulfilling thing you can do. Now, let's look at how to pass your legacy on to future generations.

Chapter 13:

Because It's How You Pass Your Legacy on to the Next Generation

We all die. The goal isn't to live forever,
the goal is to create something that will.
—Chuck Palahniuk

I was talking with a new acquaintance of mine, Terry, about the PEACE Legacy Formula and how living your life according to the formula makes living and leaving a legacy easy.

As we spoke, he shared a story with me about how his first boss, Gerald, left an indelible impact on him. "My first job out of law school was in the New York City office of a large, national law firm," Terry recalled. "As you might imagine, large law firms aren't generally known for being the most pleasant places to work. But no matter what I was dealing with, it was clear from the start that Gerald was not only willing to listen to me, but that he actually cared. And, while I didn't always get exactly what I wanted when I went to him with an issue, I always left his office feeling heard, respected, and better than when I entered."

Most people in the legal profession have little time for niceties around the office. Not Gerald. But not because of one big gesture. It was because of all the little things he did on a daily basis. He valued and built respectful relationships with everyone at the firm, from his fellow partners to brand-new attorneys and staff. Nothing special. Just living his life in natural alignment with the PEACE Legacy Formula. Terry saw the example lived out every day in front of him and vowed to do the same as he advanced in his career.

That's it. That's how we pass along legacies to the next generation. Not through some intentional "passing of the baton," so to speak, from one generation to another. And not through some formal or large organization, like a charitable organization, with systems and funding to ensure their legacy is preserved and passed along. Although both of those ways are possible. But through a natural extension of living your life as a legacy maker.

The more I looked into passing along legacies, the more I realized how simple it was. In fact, just by living intentionally as a legacy maker, you can pass along your legacy—big or small—for generations to come.

A Walk around the Block

Terry has long since left the practice of law and explored entrepreneurship, but he kept the lessons he learned from his boss and applied them to his own life as one of those natural legacy makers. He took his legacy making to another level, working intentionally to do at least one small thing under each element of the formula every day, like we talked about at the end of chapter 6. He touches base with important people in his life on a regular basis, even just to say hello, making even small interactions with him "experience-like," as he describes it. He built assets and protection for his kids and his kids' kids, developing creations, including podcasts, articles, music, online courses, and even books. And, finally, expressing kindness through his words and deeds.

One of the most remarkable observations I had in my conversations with him is how simply he created a tradition with his two children. Every day, either before school or right after dinner, he would take a short walk with each of his kids; no agenda, just a walk. At first, it wasn't easy to get his kids to leave the house. They loved spending time with him, but they had their own routines. In the beginning, the walks felt like a disruption to them. Within a short time, however, the kids began texting him at the office, asking when he'd be home, and meeting him at the door with their shoes on ready to go on their walks.

Today, his kids still want to take their walks, even when they're with their mother or grandmother, *and they talk about how much they want to do it with their families when they have kids one day.*

Legacy.

Traditions Keep Your Legacy Alive

"We have to keep the tradition alive. Game nights with dad are now game nights with family." Those two sentences sum up exactly how easy it is to keep your legacy alive. The two sentences were part of a Facebook post from someone who had recently lost her father. In the post, she included a picture of two family members playing a board game that they used to play with her late father.

What might surprise you is that the person who shared the post had lived an exceptional life. She was a multimillionaire who had built multiple seven-figure businesses and built a huge social media following. When her father passed away, she could have chosen any number of ways to keep his legacy alive. She could have started a foundation in his honor. She could have created a scholarship in his name. She could have named a room at her local public library or YMCA after him. She had the means and sophistication to do many things that would keep his memory alive.

And while she certainly might do one or more of those things over time, her post reveals that it really is simple to preserve your legacy. All you need to do is be intentional and consistent. Even a regular "game night" can become something your family and others cherish long after you pass away.

Just think back to all the little things you and your family do today that were started by your grandparents or their grandparents. Of course, they may not have meant for their habits, holiday traditions, or other small gestures to be a way to preserve their legacy, but they did. Families frequently reminisce as they cook their specialty soups, bake their desserts, or celebrate their favorite holidays. Big or small, traditions give us simple and easy ways for our legacies to pass down from one generation to another.

What's more, the best part about using traditions to preserve our legacies is that they don't require any big gestures or planning. Regularly cooking your favorite meal and sharing the recipe with family and friends gets them thinking about you even long after you're gone. As they cook, they'll naturally recall memories of experiences with you and even talk with people about you and your recipe.

Other common examples of traditions that can keep your legacy alive include the following:

1. Holiday traditions, such as hosting a special Christmas dinner

2. Daily rituals, such as eating dinner together without devices on a nightly basis

3. Weekly routines, such as Sunday church attendance or ice cream nights

4. Family activities, such as an annual charity drive that you organize

5. Hobbies, such as playing catch or collecting cards, dolls, or memorabilia

6. Shared regular experiences, such as going to sporting events, concerts, or the theater on a regular basis

Traditions turn what's important to you into habits shared by friends, family, and others.

Giving Family and Friends Stories to Share

While writing this chapter, Janice, another acquaintance of mine, who knows I'm writing this book, reached out to me excited to tell me about a social media post one of her friends shared.

The post was short, with a picture of two toddlers and a caption that simply read, "Tonight these two celebrated Grandpa Nicholas. He died many years before they were born, but he lives on in the stories we share. Paul is his string bean twin and Angela has his gentle and low-key demeanor. For this 20th anniversary, all of his people gathered to remember and celebrate a great man."

"That's it," Janice shared. "That's legacy. And, like you said, the post didn't describe some foundation or grand gesture for Grandpa Nicholas. Just 'stories to share,' followed by his 'string bean' body type and 'gentle and low-key demeanor.'"

That's so true and it's why the PEACE Legacy Formula is so important to live by intentionally and regularly. Your relationships with people ensure many people know your demeanor, what you look like, and how you treat them. Your expressions of kindness, experiences, and creations you develop will give them stories to tell and creations to share. Your assets will create many opportunities to keep your memory alive, such as by displaying memorabilia you collected or using money you left to them for school or to purchase a car or house.

Leverage Your Legacy by Connecting Your Traditions with Others

Although living intentionally by the PEACE Legacy Formula will cause you to naturally build a legacy that passes on to others, if you did want to add a little more intention to passing down or growing your legacy, you could do so by sharing what's meaningful to you in partnership with other groups.

For example, my publisher, Morgan James Publishing, has developed a formal relationship with Habitat for Humanity®, regularly supporting the organization through their book sales to help families obtain healthy, affordable places to call home.

Another friend of mine recently partnered with the Make-A-Wish® Foundation to sponsor an entire wish, including his wife and kids in the experience of choosing which wish to sponsor. He's now working to partner with an organization to help extinguish $1 million in medical debt for low-income families.

Others host golf tournaments or organize groups to participate in runs or cycling races to support causes they believe in. There are countless ways you can leverage your impact in areas that matter to you by partnering with other organizations or organizing regular group events.

You could certainly go even "bigger" and more intentional, so to speak, by creating your own organization like I did with Abundance International. But the truth is, legacy makers can, but don't need to, go big when it comes to passing along your legacy to generations. If you're consistent with living your life according to the PEACE Legacy Formula, your actions will become traditions your family and others associate with you and pass along for generations. They become a natural extension of who you were while you were alive. Even better, you won't have to wait until you pass away to see your legacy begin to take shape in other people's actions. As author, leadership expert, and motivational speaker John C. Maxwell famously said, "More is caught than taught." In other words, your actions are contagious, and it's only a matter of time before your kids host their own "game night" in their house or take walks around the block with your grandkids.

There's No Limit to How Big Your Traditions Can Grow

On February 2, 1887, locals gathered at Gobbler's Knob in Punxsutawney, Pennsylvania, in an attempt to predict whether the townspeople could expect extended winter or early spring. The townspeople watched as a groundhog came out of its hole.

This groundhog, lovingly named "Punxsutawney Phil," became the center of the tradition. The theory was that if the groundhog saw its shadow, they could expect six more weeks of winter weather. If not, they believed spring would arrive early. If you're curious, various news organizations and other websites indicate that Punxsutawney Phil's predictions have been correct approximately 39 percent of the time,[8] yet millions of people around the US still stop what they're doing every February 2 to check whether the groundhog saw its shadow, suggesting the continued celebration is much more about tradition than prediction.

Similarly, traditions in corporate settings allow companies to keep founders' and other key historical company leaders' memories alive, such as Apple's annual "Steve Jobs Day" celebration or Walmart's annual Sam Walton's birthday celebration. These types of celebrations typically honor the entrepreneurial spirits and visions of leaders and their impact on their companies, industries, and more. Sure, Steve Jobs and Sam Walton likely didn't lay out the plans to celebrate themselves before they passed. However, they left such an impact on their organizations and the world that their companies' celebrations of their lives almost seem inevitable. Of course, if you are a founder or corporate leader you certainly could create a celebration that turns into a day in your honor after you retire or pass away, although I wouldn't advise naming it after yourself while you're still alive, but a celebration to honor the value and impact of your company would be appreciated by all in your corporate family and your customers.

At the end of the day, creating traditions at home or at work that keep your memory alive and your impact growing after you pass away doesn't have to be complicated. It can be as simple as family game night or a regular walk around your neighborhood. It could be one step above that with you organizing a charitable run or hosting an annual picnic. It certainly could involve forming your own foundation or charitable organization, but it doesn't have to start big. Simply living according to the PEACE Legacy Formula on a regular basis will get you much of the way there.

---

8   See, for example: Aaron Barker, "How Accurate Is Punxsutawney Phil?," FOX Weather, February 2, 2023, accessed May 5, 2023, https://www.foxweather.com/learn/how-accurate-is-punxsutawney-phil-really. And "Groundhog Day History from Stormfax®" Stormfax, 2019, www.stormfax.com/ghogday.htm.

If you do want to get even more intentional to ensure you plant the seeds for traditions that will last for generations, just get started. Start by identifying your values and interests among family members, employees, or customers. What are some things that you all enjoy doing together? What are some values that you hold in common? Use these as a starting point for creating new traditions.

Involve as many in the planning process as you can so they feel a sense of ownership. Encourage them to share ideas and opinions, and work together to come up with a plan that everyone is excited about.

For a tradition to truly become a part of your family's culture, it's important to make it consistent. Choose a specific day or time of year to celebrate your tradition, and make sure everyone involved knows when to expect it.

Keep it simple. Traditions don't need to be complicated or expensive. In fact, some of the best traditions are the simplest ones. Focus on creating experiences that are meaningful and enjoyable for everyone.

Finally, always be flexible. Family traditions can evolve over time. As your family grows and changes, it's natural for your traditions to evolve as well. Don't be afraid to tweak your traditions as needed to keep them fresh and relevant.

If you want to build meaningful traditions in a business setting, here are some ideas that could work out well.

Celebrate key anniversaries of the company or of significant events in the company's history. For example, you might celebrate special company anniversaries, such as a two-year anniversary (because 20 percent of businesses fail within two years—celebrate making it that far), five-year anniversary (45 percent of businesses fail within five years), ten-year anniversary (65 percent of businesses fail within ten years), and so forth.[9]

---

9   U.S. Bureau of Labor Statistics (BLS) (2023). Business Employment Dynamics, Table 7: Survival of Private Sector Establishments by Opening Year.https://www.bls.gov/bdm/us_age_naics_00_table7.txt

Create company awards that recognize team members who exemplify the values and work ethic of the company's founders. Host a ceremony during which you describe the values and work ethic displayed by the winners to reinforce those principles to all employees.

If your company was founded by someone else, consider hosting a founder's day celebration like Apple and Walmart do to honor Steve Jobs and Sam Walton.

Simply put, traditions don't only apply to legacies in your personal life. Legacy makers build PEACE into their work just as much as they do in their personal lives. And there's no reason they can't build traditions in their work life to pass along their legacy to another generation.

Creating meaningful traditions that support the values and history of a company and its founders requires creativity, thoughtfulness, and a deep understanding of the company's culture and history. By investing in these traditions, companies can strengthen their sense of identity, inspire employees, and create a lasting legacy.

Chapter 14:

Because It's the Bridge to the Eternal You

We are not human beings having a spiritual experience;
we are spiritual beings having a human experience.
—Pierre Teilhard de Chardin

This chapter is an adventurous step into the great beyond: the spirit realm. Most people would agree that we, as human beings, are a beautiful integration of body, mind, and spirit. It's easy to see how your body is real. Additionally, you listen to thousands of your own thoughts each day, so your mind is definitely real. But do you have any idea what your spirit is like or how it exists as part of you? Few take the idea seriously or strive to discover their true identity: the Eternal You.

What is your true identity? If I were to ask you to tell me a bit about yourself, you'd probably tell me your name and about your family. You'd tell me what you do for a living and where you live. All of these are true statements, but is it who you truly are?

When I was eighteen, I worked at Hume Lake Christian Camps for the summer after high school. It occurred to me that no one there would know me, so I thought I'd shake it up a bit and go by the name Steve. And it worked! My name badge said Steve and that's what I was called by everyone. Why wouldn't they? It's how I introduced myself and what my name badge read. Even though I was called Steve, was I still me? Of course! Obviously, who I am more is than my name.

Additionally, I've had numerous professions, lived in different places, and experienced family changes. Was it still me in all of those differing roles? Again, yes, of course. Well then, who am I really?

Perhaps I am my thoughts and emotions? Those seemed to stay with me. I would have continued to think so until one day when I was assisting Dr. Robert Glover at a men's retreat. He had us do a meditation exercise. After a few deep breaths, he asked us to do an inventory of ourselves. He instructed, "Now, as the nonjudgmental observer of yourself, notice how your body is feeling." He had us go slowly from our head to feet and just feel and observe. Then we did the same with our emotions. What are we feeling? Are there resentments hiding in the back of our minds? Fears? Anger? Happiness? Then he asked us to allow our thoughts to flow in front of our awareness. Are there patterns of thoughts that are circling? Are there some thoughts that repeat? Often we shy away from looking at thoughts that bother us, but these are just our thoughts. No one else is seeing them. Why not let them flow and observe? We spent about fifteen minutes in this exercise and observed ourselves on various levels without judgment. It was a really interesting exercise for everyone involved.

Then, this question hit me. If I can observe my thoughts and emotions, who is doing the observing? Obviously, I'm not my thoughts or emotions if I can independently observe them. So then, who am I really? Was this my spirit doing the observing? My conclusion is that it was. I am certainly not the first to come to this realization, but it was new to me and very profound.

I doubt that you need much convincing that you have a spirit or that there is a spirit realm. Perhaps you too have had similar experiences to these examples. Have you ever been apart from a loved one and the both of you text each other simultaneously? How did you both know to write at that very same moment if you're not connected by your spirits? Have you felt stressed and they called you wondering whether you were OK because they just *felt* that something was wrong? Can your spirit really connect with someone irrespective of distance? I believe that it is very obvious that it can.

Have you ever had an intuition about something you shouldn't have known, but it proved true? Or maybe you ignored that still, small voice within you and your decision backfired? How many times have you said to yourself, "I knew I shouldn't have done that, but I did it anyway and wish I'd listened to myself." Which "self" did you wish you'd listened to? Who was that still, small voice that was speaking to you?

Conclusively, I think we can acknowledge that we have a spirit—and most of us wish we could hear it more clearly and listen more often! So, how does your spirit work with you, and what does this have to do with your eternal legacy? Who is the Eternal You?

I'm going to take a risk and share a very personal story of an unusual and special experience. I've since learned that many have had similar experiences, including Dr. Jordan Peterson.[10] I can't think of a better way to explain this mystery than with this story.

I was spending a few days with a good friend of mine who was also a personal development coach. As he shared with me some of his teachings on releasing pains from the past, he encouraged me to go into a meditation and listen to my heart for what truly needs to be healed, so I did.

I was lying comfortably on pillows on the floor and listening to some great music from Brazil. An hour passed and nothing had come to me, but the calm was pleasant.

Another hour passed when suddenly a thought, or voice, or message spoke and asked me, "Have you forgiven God yet?" I was startled by it, sat

---

10 Jordan Peterson, "Q & A 2018 08 August B," YouTube, August 14, 2017, https://www. youtube.com/watch?v=MeNxc6MqXuM&t=1435s.

up, and said out loud, "What?" But I knew exactly what was being asked, and it wasn't something I'd even thought about for more than a decade. Years earlier, my second wife had passed away. At the time, I hadn't intellectually blamed God, but obviously a part of me had. I stopped going to church. I withdrew spiritually in many ways.

Forgive God? Until that moment I didn't realize how attached I'd become to this unconscious resentment. I had to laugh at the lunacy of hearing a question that I'd never really considered before. But it was spot on. For the next hour, I wrestled with this thought. I didn't want to let go of my deep resentment. Finally, a sense of peace came over me and I quietly spoke, "God, I let go of my unforgiveness toward you." It was a good first step, but I could sense that this wasn't enough. I knew he wanted me to open my heart and ask him to be part of my life journey again; welcoming him as I would a friend. I wrestled more with this next step before finally warming my heart to invite him to come. A deep sense of peace came. It was done. And I truly did want to have a relationship with him again.

Suddenly, in that moment of openness, I had a dream or visualization. I honestly don't know which it was, nor does it matter. What would come next would change my life forever. I saw the ceiling open to space or the spirit realm and a bright spirit came flowing toward me. I felt love and joy coming from him and a big smile on his face. He didn't introduce himself, but I somehow knew it was the Holy Spirit.

He spoke to me and asked, "Would you allow me to borrow your spirit so we can dance?" I was completely dumbstruck by what I was seeing and what was being asked. I tried to gather myself together enough to give an intelligent answer. "But if I let my spirit go, won't I die?" The spirit smiled more and replied, "No. You have a strong body. You'll be fine. It will only be for a few minutes." And with that, he reached out toward me, and I saw my spirit rise out of the top of my head and the two danced, spinning in a euphoric circle of joy! I could feel the energy of complete love and excitement between them! I remember thinking that the elation was so great it was as if they'd been waiting to see each other for thousands of years and were overjoyed to finally be reconnected. It was breathtaking. Beautiful.

As they danced together, this thought came to me: "Wait. That's my spirit! That's me! I am loved! And I am one of them! My eternal home is there! That's where I belong!"

A few minutes later, my spirit returned to me, and the Holy Spirit drifted back to where he first came. Again, trying to make sense of this and respond intelligently, I said to my spirit, "You seemed so happy. Do you want to go? I don't want to keep you trapped here with me if you'd rather be there." My spirit laughed and said, "What are you talking about? I am you! It's all good, believe me."

Before the opening in the ceiling closed, I was given one last vision. I could see millions, perhaps billions, of spirits spinning around a bright center of light energy; it was the Source of love and the Creator of all that is. It looked like how you would imagine seeing a galaxy spinning in a slow rotation. I could feel the love and excitement holding them together in this huge celebration. And, at the center was the Source, or God himself. Then it was over.

As I lay there on the floor stunned, eyes staring blankly at the ceiling, I felt amazing love holding me like a warm blanket. Why me? What had I done to deserve such a beautiful experience? I'm still in awe of it all to this day.

Since I grew up in a pastor's home, I knew much of the Bible. But I now began to understand new insights into these things I'd grown up with. It all had fresh meaning. I'll share two of those insights with you in a minute.

Whether you want to believe this vision as literal or not, there are some paradigm-shifting insights that come from it including new understandings about our spirits that I want to share.

Before I go any further, let me offer a few clarifications and definitions of terms. This vision was given to me in a way that I needed for my own spiritual growth. As I heard more and more about others who had visions, each was a bit different, but the essence of the experiences seemed to be similar in this way; they all felt intense love and union as part of that world. I will talk about my "spirit" because that's how I would describe this part of myself. Others refer to their higher self, soul, the deep "I," or a quiet presence. Some like to use the terms God, the universe, or their higher power. I will refer to him as the Source of all that is, or God. I say "him" even though it was clear to me that neither he, nor any spirit, has a gender. I'll ask you to hold off on any attachments to words, judgments, or labels and just listen quietly within to what truth may be here for you.

The first takeaway is that we all have a spirit—a literal spirit. I think I'd only given an intellectual nod to this notion in the past, but now it was very real. I also understood clearly that my spirit is already connected to all wisdom and love from the Source of all that is. I am one with him and all of my fellow spirits. I also know that I am deeply loved and accepted right now. My eternal family is there for me and that will be home when my time in this earth suit is done because my spirit is already there and one with that world. That's not a small thing. In fact, it's probably the greatest truth imaginable. This is our true identity. We are eternal spirit beings experiencing human existence during our time here.

I believe that there will come a time in that other world when we'll see each other and reflect on what we did with our time here. We'll fondly share stories of how we tried to help each other while on our journeys here.

I knew for certain that I had a real spirit, who is one with the Source of infinite knowledge, love, and wisdom. I wanted to learn how to be more connected and listen.

To help explain how you can connect better with your spirit, and the heart of God, or Source, allow me to share two new insights I received that first day, which came from the story of Adam and Eve.

The story of Adam and Eve is a foundational part of the leading world religions, as well as many other tribal ancestral stories. As you know from the story, a serpent came to pose a challenge to them. I say the challenge was posed to both of them because, even though it says the conversation was with Eve, it also says that her husband was right there with her the whole time. Allow me to paraphrase the conversation. First the serpent asks Eve, "Has God really given you everything you need?" Eve responds that he has. Then, the serpent challenges further, "God doesn't want you to eat from that one tree because it will give you the same knowledge of good and evil as he has. He's holding out on you." They both ate the fruit and immediately realized they were naked.

OK, that much you know, but what struck me on reading this again was a seemingly obvious question, yet one I'd not considered before: "How could they have lived there for years, walked in the garden with God in the afternoons, and suddenly now realize that they were naked?" Allow me to propose a hypothesis. I believe that prior to that moment, they had lived primarily in their spirits, more than their bodies. The Scripture says that God is spirit, and perhaps that was their primary form of being as well. Perhaps, at the moment when they "sinned," they were cut off from their own spirits and only then clearly realized, for the first time, how naked their bodies were. If so, then their lives in their spirits may have been so real that their bodies were less consequential. And, in the very same way, today we are completely living in our bodies and have very little recognition of our spirits at all. We are all created uniquely with bodies, minds, *and* spirits. We've just lost touch with our spirits and lived in this fallen condition of just mind and body for thousands of years.

Today, the hearts of people everywhere have begun to long to be reunited with their spirits. It's a deep desire placed in the hearts of everyone. I also believe that we're experiencing a spiritual awakening around the world right now and millions of people are beginning to reconnect with their spirits and with God.

However, since we have only experienced life from our "thinking bodies," as I call it, how can we be reunited with our spirits again? The Scripture offers us a clue to answer this question. In Psalm 46:10 God says, "Be still, and know that I am God" (New International Version). It is in the stillness that we can hear from him and what our own spirit is trying to tell us.

Stillness requires getting above thought. This is where meditation comes in, as we covered previously. Monks know this skill, as does anyone who seeks to hear from the Source. As you become more skilled at quieting your mind and listening, you'll find that place of peace and calm. Insights will follow. You'll make better decisions and be more loving. In time, you'll learn to live in this state as you go throughout your day and not just while in meditation.

One concluding insight I think you'll appreciate is this. In that story, I personally don't think that the original sin was when they ate the fruit. Rather, it came just before that. When the serpent asked Eve whether God had truly been taking care of them, her first response was, and I will paraphrase, "Yes! God has totally taken care of us! Have you seen this place? It's a paradise! We have everything we could ever want!" To which the serpent replied, "Oh, really? Did he give you everything? What about that tree over there he told you not to eat from? He didn't really give you everything, did he?" In the moment that they questioned whether God had given them everything they needed or not, they broke the heart of God and only then acted on their doubts by taking that bite. But the sin was when they went from gratitude to doubt.

Why is this important? Every faith on the planet, every self-help expert, and everyone who wants to grow, has acknowledged the value of a gratitude practice. Why? Because this pleases the heart of the Source of all that is. For us to turn to him and declare by faith, "I believe you have already given me everything I truly need in this life" brings abundance, peace, and manifestations.

Even Jesus instructed us to pray in this way in Mark 11:24: "Therefore I tell you, whatever you ask in prayer, believe that you have already received it, and it will be yours" (New International Version). Do you believe that you already have everything you truly need? Or do you find yourself complaining about what you don't have and think you need? Do you believe that whatever you need has already been given to you from the generous and loving Source of all that is? This is a real struggle for many of us who have put so much energy and focus on our challenges. That's all we tend to see. And where focus goes, energy flows, as we discussed previously.

Perhaps you've had a cynical view of the universe up until now. Yet even Albert Einstein has said, "The most important decision we make is whether we believe we live in a friendly or hostile universe." You may need some internal healing from bad representations you've had before, about God or the universe, but this is where all spiritual abundance begins. In your gratitude practice, believe that God has already provided you with everything you need and thank him for it daily.

The Eternal You is loved. The Eternal You is one with the Source of all that is, even now. The Eternal You has no lack, and neither does the earthly you.

Your time on earth in your thinking body is limited, but it is a gift. The angels were not given such an opportunity to experience a life in this world as you have been. Be grateful for every experience you can have here; appreciate every sunset. See the beauty all around you. Feel the presence of God in every living thing as if it were all made just for you. Pause for a moment to absorb that thought. If you weren't here, this world would not matter, so why not assume it was all here for you to enjoy? As with any gift, the giver hopes for you to enjoy it to the fullest.

Understand this, your purpose here includes being able to someday recollect your stories with your fellow spirits. At first, I worried about this idea. Would some of my fellow spirits also remember when I was not kind to them? Based on what we are told, no, that's not part of our eternal experience. Scripture tells us that there will be no tears in the Kingdom of Heaven—the spirit realm. From my experience, and the countless others who have said they encountered the spirit realm, the stories are strikingly similar; it is a realm governed by an overwhelming sense of love and joy. There is no sense of lack, guilt, remorse, or loss. But, how cool will it be to meet fellow spirits that we did some good for who would share the stories with us from their perspective? And many of them we never met in this life! What you do here will matter there.

From this new perspective, I hope you'll see your fellow humans also as fellow spirits on the same journey with you and already united with you in spirit. Keep this view in mind as you interact with everyone.

I completely acknowledge that what any of us do in our human forms will not be as healthy as it could be if we were more connected with our spirits. We are still deeply flawed here; as is everyone else you will encounter. You will need to forgive and be understanding as part of your daily life. But showing love to others, and yourself, is the right thing to do from the perspective of the Eternal You. You don't show love so they will be grateful to you, although some will. That only feeds the ego of your thinking body. You show love and understanding because your heart will want to, and because you'll connect with them later and they'll celebrate with you.

Can you imagine a world where everyone understands that all of our spirits are already united as one? Would you see people differently? Treat them differently? If love is the essence of the spirit realm, could we make it the predominant way we conduct our lives in this world as well?

Why did I dedicate a chapter to this topic in a book on legacies? Because the greatest enemy of significance is indifference. In other words, you might ask yourself, "Why would it matter what I do here once I'm gone? Who cares if the kids fight over my stuff? I won't be here. It won't matter to me." This may sound like a very cynical argument, especially after everything you've read so far, but I've had these same thoughts in the past. I think we all have. But it saddens me to know that many won't understand that there is an Eternal You until they are there. They will see no purpose in leaving anything behind once they're gone because they "won't be here." Furthermore, their only motivation in this life will be to feed the egos of their thinking bodies with self-interests and self-indulgences. Be patient with them and love them anyway.

I wanted to add this chapter, among other reasons, to answer the futility of thinking with indifference. My takeaway from this chapter is this: What you do here matters and life can be filled with more love, reward, and satisfaction than you imagine. Live with the understanding that your true self, your spirit, is united with the Source, and you have been given everything you need, even the desires of your heart are available to you. View your fellow humans as spirit travelers with you even now. Your acts of service will be remembered for all time, and your heart can be filled with love.

I'm not saying that the other realm will be anything like this one, especially when we are told that there will be no tears there, and the environment has been characterized by love. And, in that place, we will know and be known by each other instantly. The apostle Paul compared our current life with the one to come in this way in 1 Corinthians 13:12: "For presently we see through a glass in obscurity; but then, face to face. Presently, I know in part; but then I will know fully, even as I have been fully known" (Berean Literal Translation). Further, Jesus said in John 10:10, "The thief's purpose is to steal and kill and destroy. My purpose is to give them a rich and satisfying life" (New Living Translation). It was important to the Source that we have a richly satisfying life here. Let's make it important to us as well.

This whole chapter may be a bit too much for some. I knew that going into it. If that's you, I know that the rest of the book is still filled with more than enough value to make reading it worthwhile. Your life can be richly satisfying and in a way that you too will leave your legacy. It's worth your time to learn how to live out the PEACE Legacy Formula on its merits alone. If that is you, then let this chapter go and build your legacy with all of the tools here. For others, this was a new paradigm that can bring joy, peace, and desire to connect more with the Source of all that is, and more with their own eternal spirit.

I look forward to connecting with you there if we don't meet here first.

Conclusion and Invitation

The World Belongs to the Legacy Makers

You Either Leave a Legacy or You Leave a Hole

I could have written this entire book about how personally fulfilling it is to spend your days focusing on the PEACE elements in the Legacy Formula, as each element is designed to bring joy in the present and peace of mind for the future.

The truth is, it's not hard to see how personally fulfilling the journey of becoming a legacy maker can be when you pause even for a moment to reflect on what life would be like if you were living the PEACE elements on a day-to-day basis.

Even beyond that, however, there are few joys greater than knowing that you matter and are making a difference in the world. And there's no way to fully describe how valuable you are. Valuable to me, to your friends and loved ones, and even to people you have never met (and may never meet) but whose lives become better because of your contributions.

When the day comes that you leave your body behind for what lies ahead, one of two things will happen: you will leave a legacy or you will leave a hole.

If you leave a legacy

- stories about you will be passed down for generations from people who call you a mentor, friend, loving parent, and more;
- the experiences you shared with people will continue to ripple throughout their families, friends, and communities;
- the assets you created will protect your family and others and will continue to grow and impact the world;
- the creations you share with others will keep your talents, thoughts, and messages alive and can touch millions you may never even meet; and
- the kindness you expressed while you are here will leave a lasting legacy on the people who benefited from your kindness and others, as the people you impacted will carry the torch of kindness you lit before your passing.

If you don't intentionally build a legacy, however, you will leave a hole of "what could have been." It's a gap that will be left for others to fill if that's even possible.

What could have been if you had the courage to build, deepen, or repair important relationships? What could have been if you had said "yes" to the opportunity to share meaningful experiences with family, friends, and others beyond your immediate circle? What could have been if you had built and safeguarded assets to preserve for people you loved? What could have been if you had shared creations that recorded your talents, thoughts, and messages for others? And what could have been had you expressed kindness to others, making them feel more loved and inspiring them to pay all that kindness forward to others?

But your story will not end with a question. The last chapter in the book of *your* life won't end with wonder about what could have been.

You're a legacy maker now. And from this day forward, you will get to experience tremendous joy and fulfillment as you build your legacy and become the fullest version of yourself possible.

The world needs you and your gifts. Your fellow legacy makers need your help. We need your presence and energy. We need you to live your destiny, of a life rich in experiences beyond your wildest dreams. There is no way to replace your contributions on this earth, either, because you are uniquely you. Nobody can share your heart the way you do just like nobody can share the messages I'm sharing here exactly as I'm doing it.

You were given beautiful gifts to share. And if you start, stay values-driven, and continue even when the inevitable obstacles you will face appear, you will touch people in ways no one imagined.

There is no life like that of a legacy maker. It's yours for the taking. And when you do, you'll never want to live any other way again.

You were chosen to be alive at this time for a reason.

To make the most of the limited amount of time we all have here on earth.

To work intentionally and not let the busyness of daily life, going through the motions, and just trying to get by get in the way.

But it takes intention to create this kind of life. It requires us to be intentional with our time, to prioritize the things that truly matter, and to make the most of every moment we have.

The world needs you. We need you to follow your heart, your passion, your calling. We need you to take action and not accept that your current situation is all there is.

Imagine for a moment how all of our lives would be different today *if*

- Nelson Mandela gave up hope while he was in prison
- Steve Jobs just sulked after leaving Apple the first time and never did another thing
- Princess Diana was just happy enjoying all the benefits of being a royal and never left the palace

- Steven Spielberg never made a movie
- Anne Sullivan didn't have the patience to teach Helen Keller

How big of a hole would each of them have created? What could have been?

But we don't have to answer that question for each of these people because they took action. We know what could have been because we've all benefited from the contributions they made.

But contributions don't need to be on a global scale to make an impact. You don't need to be Steve Jobs or Princess Diana to be a legacy maker. Just think back to the people who touched your life.

- Was it a school teacher who made an impact on you?
- Perhaps a boss encouraged you on your career path.
- Maybe you launched a business and someone believed in you.
- Or, maybe, when you were at your lowest, a good friend never left your side.

"Regular" people just like you and me build and leave legacies on a daily basis. And, when we follow the PEACE Legacy Formula for doing so, we get to see and feel the impact of our efforts in real time.

We get to experience the emotional rush and personal fulfillment of having relationships with people, enjoying our experiences, building our assets, sharing our creations, and expressing kindness while we are still here.

Final Thoughts and an Invitation

You're in for the ride of your life and the life of your dreams. Thank you for allowing me to be part of your journey.

You're part of us now, a loyal community of legacy makers, and I want to make sure we stay connected. First, I'd love to hear from you personally. Shoot me an email and let me know what points in the book resonated with you and what you'll be doing now going forward. Write to me at marcum@marcumdavis.com.

Second, go to MarcumDavis.com and get on the email list for regular words of encouragement, insights, tips, strategies, and ways to be an active part of this movement. Perhaps we can be of help to you in developing your legacy plan.

I invite you to become an active part of the community of other like-minded legacy makers. We are changing the world together.

Finally, please pick up extra copies of *Legacy* to share with everyone around you. The world needs a shift in consciousness and we can do it together.

This is the greatest life I could imagine, and I know it will be for you too as you live out your legacy today. Welcome to the great adventure!

My best to you always,

About the "Spirit Warrior" Symbol

In short, the message behind the Spirit Warrior symbol is this: "We are called to be skilled and able to protect and defend what is important to us, and spiritually aware of the needs around us."

The sword represents sharpened skills. The term "meek" in ancient Greek, as Jesus used it when he said, "Blessed are the meek, for they shall inherit the earth," is a reference to a person who is skilled with the sword but chooses to keep it sheathed in discipline and restraint. Knowing you have the skills and willingness to defend what is important to you, and choosing to live in peace as much as it is up to you, is the power that can inherit the earth.

The Spartan helmet is a symbol of discipline and self-sacrifice. It's our willingness to be dedicated to the good of our community.

The top part of the sword represents royalty. It reminds us that we are children of the King, the One who is all and in all.

The wings represent the union with our own spirit and the continual awareness of the needs around us.

I hope you resonate with this symbol. I invite you to make it your personal symbol as well. For me, I've incorporated it into the armor tattoos I wear proudly. You don't have to make it into a tattoo, although that would be cool, but send me a picture of you with the book as you travel, or you with some merchandise item you pick up from our site. It would be encouraging to me to see more people embrace the message behind the symbol.

We are all called to be spirit warriors and spirit workers in this world.

About Abundance International

I loved those years before the war because of how delightful it was to interact with the children in these orphanages in Ukraine. With each food delivery or construction project, we would spend time playing with a room of kids and could feel their openness as they crawled onto our laps to be held.

To see them having to adapt to living in bomb shelters was heartbreaking. The needs were great and we did what we could, and we continue to do what we can, because of donations from people like you.

All author royalties from this book go directly to Abundance International, and I'd welcome your partnering with us as well.

Please visit AbundanceInternational.org to learn more about what we're doing around the world today.

Abundance
International, Inc.

Appreciation

One is too small a number to achieve greatness.
—JOHN C. MAXWELL

Bringing all of these thoughts to paper was a beautiful venture with my friend, editor, and writing partner, Nick Pavlidis (NickPavlidis.com). I'm grateful for your brilliance and insights into the publishing world. It's all reflected here. You rock.

To David Hancock, publisher at Morgan James Publishing, I've been so impressed with you, and everyone at Morgan James. I felt that the success of this book was assured with your help.

To Rachel Johnson, Rick's daughter. Thank you for allowing me to share your father's story as such an inspirational part of this book. He was dearly loved and left a legacy that I am proud to have honored in this book.

To my dearest friends Dr. Robert Glover and Brian Begin. You've been with me through so many adventurous experiences, and I treasure them all.

To my brother, Keith Davis. Thank you for everything you've done for me and our parents. Your guidance and support have been so valuable especially during those early days of the war. Strength and honor.

Finally, to all of those who work and have worked for me in Ukraine and the staff and volunteers at Abundance International. You are true heroes, and I hope to share more of your stories in the future.

About the Author

Marcum Davis is a well-known entrepreneur, speaker, and author in personal development, the non-profit sector, spirit-based living, and relationship coaching. He is the founder of Abundance International, a nonprofit corporation supporting orphanages in Ukraine since 2012.

Before starting Abundance International, Davis had a successful career in the computer industry. However, after experiencing a personal crisis in the 2008 crash, he decided to shift his focus to helping others create their legacies and more meaningful relationships.

Davis was a sought-after philanthropist during the early stages of the Russian invasion because of his work with the orphanages in Ukraine. He has been featured in numerous media outlets, including the BBC, CNN, Fox News, NBC, MSNBC, ABC, CBS, and many others.

He is passionate about helping people find their purpose and create their own legacies.

A free ebook edition is available with the purchase of this book.

To claim your free ebook edition:

1. Visit MorganJamesBOGO.com
2. Sign your name CLEARLY in the space
3. Complete the form and submit a photo of the entire copyright page
4. You or your friend can download the ebook to your preferred device

Morgan James BOGO™

A **FREE** ebook edition is available for you or a friend with the purchase of this print book.

CLEARLY SIGN YOUR NAME ABOVE

Instructions to claim your free ebook edition:
1. Visit MorganJamesBOGO.com
2. Sign your name CLEARLY in the space above
3. Complete the form and submit a photo of this entire page
4. You or your friend can download the ebook to your preferred device

Print & Digital Together Forever.

Snap a photo

Free ebook

Read anywhere